TENNIS

Wayne Pearce
Janice Pearce

TENNIS

Prentice-Hall, Inc., Englewood Cliffs, New Jersey

C-13-903443-9
P-13-903435-8

Library of Congress Catalog Card Number 79-149307

Printed in the United States of America

Current Printing (last digit):

12 11 10 9 8 7 6

PRENTICE-HALL, INTERNATIONAL, INC. *London*
PRENTICE-HALL OF AUSTRALIA, PTY. LTD., *Sydney*
PRENTICE-HALL OF CANADA, LTD., *Toronto*
PRENTICE-HALL OF INDIA PRIVATE LIMITED, *New Delhi*
PRENTICE-HALL OF JAPAN, INC., *Tokyo*

CONTENTS

I
The
First
Step

v

7

THE MECHANICAL BASIS OF TENNIS   61

Angles of Rebound and Spin 61   Linear and Rotatory Motion 62   Range of Motion 64   Leverage 64

8

THE DEVELOPMENT OF MOTOR SKILL   66

Perceptual-motor Aspects of Skill Development 66 Factors Affecting the Learning Situation 68   *Motivation* 68   *Preparatory set* 68   *Reinforcement* 68 *Feedback* 69   *Mental practice* 69   *Practice schedules* 70

9

CONDITIONING FOR TENNIS   72

General Physical Conditioning 72   *Ground strokes* 73   *Serving and returning drills* 73   *Volley and overhead drills* 74

10

ADVANCED STROKES AND STRATEGY   76

Advanced Strokes 76   *The half volley* 76   *The lob* 77   *The overhead smash* 78   *The drop shot* 78 *The serve* 79   Court Position and Basic Strategy 83 *Basic strategy for the novice* 83   *Position for singles play* 84   *Advance to the net on good shots* 85 *Positioning for doubles* 85   Use Your Head in Tennis 86   *Percentage tennis* 87   *Selecting a pattern of play* 88

GLOSSARY OF TERMS   91

TENNIS

The
First
Step

1

THE PARTICIPANT
AND THE CHALLENGE

This chapter will introduce you to:
1. The physiological, psychological, and motor
capacity requirement of tennis
2. The increased demands of more advanced levels of skill

Tennis is a game played by people of all ages and of all skill levels. Courts are filling with more and more players as individuals come to realize the value of tennis as a leisure-time activity, the relationship of physical exercise to health, and the satisfaction of participation. In addition, tennis is becoming a year-round activity as indoor courts are developed to supplement the traditional outdoor arrangement.

You may be one of many who have watched players on a court and responded by wanting to try the game yourself. Or you may have played previously and want to develop your skills further. In either case, it is worth looking at the problems related to the game of tennis to give you a realistic perspective of the challenge it provides.

WHO CAN PLAY TENNIS?

Few games are as suited to a variety of participants as is tennis. Tennis can be played by youngsters of seven or eight; it is a challenge to the physical prowess of the developing adolescent boy or girl; it is an activity that has achieved cultural acceptance for the young woman that is yet unseen by several other sports in American society; and it is not unusual to see men and women in their late seventies playing with sufficient skill to give younger opponents some cause for concern. Tennis can be played by men and women, either separately or together; it can be enjoyed by the unskilled as well as by the highly skilled; it necessitates only one other person, and if another player is not available, an individual can derive some benefit and enjoyment from hitting the ball against a backboard. In addition, tennis is relatively inexpensive once the initial investment in a racket has been made.

Because tennis is a game for all ages and all skill levels, it is fast becoming the nation's family sport. In a country where the family relationship has suffered from the social changes of prolonged industrialization, an activity in which members of a family can participate together has considerable merit.

Physiological Requirements

Tennis requires little physical conditioning from the beginner. People can begin to play with minimal levels of cardio-respiratory endurance. However, sufficient arm, shoulder, and wrist strength is necessary to support the racket throughout the strokes and to maintain the necessary resistance as the ball contacts the racket. Problems with beginners may occasionally relate to extremely low levels of arm strength. As skill develops, however, the physiological demands also increase, until, with the highly skilled competitor, strength, muscular endurance, cardio-respiratory endurance, and some degree of flexibility are essential factors in winning play. Training regimens, based on work with weights and a variety of running drills, are followed by tournament competitors in addition to their regular practice sessions on the court.

Tennis is an active game, however, even for the beginner, and it becomes increasingly more active as skill develops. It is a suggested activity for the player who likes to move and who enjoys physical exertion.

Motor Capacity Requirements

It would not be realistic to say that tennis is easy to master. Tennis offers a challenge far more complicated in its initial stages than do many other sports activities. It involves a series of complex motor skills; individuals walk onto a tennis court, perhaps for the first time, and are surprised at their inability to hit the ball successfully. They achieve little satisfaction from hitting it into the net one time, into a neighboring court another time, and occasionally over the back fence.

Tennis involves hitting a target moving at varying rates of speed. The target is not moving in an expected, narrow path, as, for example, a softball or baseball pitch does, but anywhere within the court area. This uncertainty of location imposes the necessity of judging the speed of the ball, the direction of its flight, and the height of its bounce. At the same time, it requires making constant spatial adjustments to position oneself for each stroke. In addition, considerable control of the muscles through the forearm and wrist is required to handle the weight of the tennis racket and to cope with the momentum and impact of the tennis ball as it contacts the racket during the swing. Thus tennis makes intensive demands on the potential performer in the area of motor ability, especially with respect to agility, balance, power, reaction time, and coordination. Speed is not as important as reaction time, court position, and the ability to anticipate your opponent's shots.

Psychological Requirements

Tennis provides many challenges—a challenge to master physical skills, a challenge to control one's responses in a variety of changing situations, and a challenge to better an opponent through the knowledge and implementation of the tools of the game.

Tennis requires constant mental alertness and perception in order to make split-second decisions. In addition, it provides the opportunity to judge the soundness of the decisions made by the play which results. A chain of cause and effect relationships can be seen with each exchange.

Many people believe that proficiency in tennis can be developed over a period of two or three months. Because of the complexity of the skills involved, however, it usually takes a longer period of time to attain proficiency in tennis than to attain equal proficiency in many other activities. This fact means that you must have a positive mental attitude toward learning the game. In order to progress beyond the raw beginner stage, considerable time and effort is necessary.

REQUIREMENTS FOR ADVANCED SKILL LEVELS

As the level of skill at which you play and the competitive level on which you play increase, so do the physical demands of the game. A beginning player spends much of his game time standing or walking, with occasional sprints of running. At an advanced level the ball is kept in play longer; it is generally hit with more force and travels faster; and it is directed away from the opponent. These differences make greater physical demands on the participant. Comparatively greater muscular endurance through the arms and legs is required to sustain play over a period of time. Greater cardio-vascular endurance is needed to respond to the demands of more movement, faster movement, and additional power. Agility, or the ability to make sudden and rapid changes of direction, becomes essential in the backcourt as well as in the volleying position near the net. To attain maximum force from a stroke it is essential to hit from a well-balanced position; thus movement and footwork assume a more important role.

Greater muscular strength is also required for advanced play. The serve of a novice does not depend on strength; control is the primary consideration. As power is attained, muscular strength becomes more significant; a powerful serve requires strength not only of arm and shoulder muscles, but also of those muscles through the back and chest. However, even in serves clocked at well over 100 miles per hour, it is a combination of strength plus a sequential, coordinated movement that produces the power. Thus, the smooth coordinated functioning of body parts is another factor essential to the advanced player.

Fast reaction time and movement time are vital to the success of the highly skilled player. Reaction time is the interval between the stimulus—the approaching tennis ball—and the beginning of muscular response. Movement time refers to adjustments in position and the stroke. A part of a player's ability to react quickly relates to the automatic or subconscious use of the cues discussed in Chapter 8. A player who is in the proper position for every hit—well balanced and prepared for the approaching ball—has good anticipation. He is aware of the position of his opponent on the court, of the angle of his opponent's racket face, of the type of stroke his opponent is making. These factors are clues to where the ball will be hit, the speed of the ball, and whether spin will be imparted. He is consequently able to begin moving into position more quickly than the player who relies only on the approaching ball. Thus reaction and movement patterns in tennis are a combination of the physiological responses of nervous tissue and the learned use of cues.

CONTRAINDICATIONS

Because tennis is a vigorous activity requiring a great deal of movement, any physical limitation preventing participation in vigorous physical activity usually rules out competitive tennis. Generally speaking, however, any person in reasonably good health can play tennis at some level of competition compatible with his age, fitness level, and skill level.

AFTER READING THIS CHAPTER, YOU SHOULD KNOW THAT:

Tennis can be played by individuals of all ages and all skill levels.

Tennis does not require a high level of physical conditioning from the beginning player; however, as skill develops, the physical demands of the game increase.

Tennis consists of a series of highly complex motor skills, and thus it may require more time to achieve a playing proficiency in tennis than in many other activities.

2

EQUIPMENT
AND FACILITIES

*After completing this chapter, you should be able
to discuss the following points:*
1. *How to select a tennis racket*
2. *Differences in quality and playing characteristics
   of various strings*
3. *Differences in tennis balls*
4. *Appropriate dress for tennis*
5. *Playing characteristics of different court surfaces*
6. *The indoor tennis court*

THE RACKET

Fig. 2-1 is a diagram of a tennis racket. You should know the names of the various parts since reference to them will be made frequently when discussing strokes.

The three basic factors which should be considered when selecting a tennis racket are the weight of the racket, the size of the grip, and the type of strings with which the racket is strung.

Tennis rackets vary in weight from 12 to 15 ounces and are classified as light, medium, and heavy. To the novice that small range may not be significant, but if a person tried swinging a 15-ounce racket after playing with a 12-ounce racket, it is safe to suggest that it might seem somewhat like swinging a baseball bat!

In selecting a tennis racket, remember that the heavier the striking implement, the greater the force which can be applied to an object by that implement, if factors such as the length of the

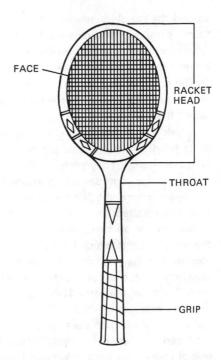

FACE

RACKET
HEAD

THROAT

GRIP

FIGURE 2-1. The racket

striking lever and the speed of the swing are held constant. Therefore, the heavier the racket, the greater the force which can be applied to the ball. However, as the weight of the racket increases, it becomes more difficult to control the swing. The problem, then, is to select as heavy a racket as can be used comfortably and without muscular fatigue or loss of control. Too light a racket, although easy to swing, does not give the desired power; too heavy a racket tires a player quickly and may cause soreness through the arm, shoulder, and possibly the back.

The following are helpful guidelines. Most women players select rackets weighing 13 to 13½ ounces. Young boys use rackets of that same weight, but a man of average size and strength should use at least a 13½-ounce racket, and most men prefer one of 13¾ or 14 ounces.

"Grip" on a tennis racket refers to the circumference of the handle and, to a lesser extent, to the shape of the handle. Rackets come in several grip sizes, and the one to use depends on one's hand size. If the handle is too small, the racket tends to slip in the hand; if it is too large, it cannot be gripped as firmly and it becomes difficult to change quickly from a forehand to a backhand grip. One way to determine grip size is to wrap the fingers around the handle in one direction and the thumb in the other direction. The thumb should extend over the first knuckle of the middle finger. This, by the way, is only a method of estimating grip size; it is not the proper way to hold a tennis racket for any of the strokes.

The grip can also vary in shape from almost round to nearly square. Most players prefer a handle a little on the square side with defined corners to give more "feel" to the grip.

In addition to weight and grip size, the balance of a racket is also a factor of its playing quality. Most players avoid a racket which is either head-heavy or handle-heavy. They prefer a racket with even balance. An approximation of the balance point can be determined by placing a finger under the racket at the point where the handle joins the head of the racket. If the weight is evenly distributed, the racket should balance at that point.

No chapter on tennis equipment would be complete without reference to the metal rackets which have achieved some popularity in recent years. The idea of a metal racket is not new. They were tried some years ago and presented problems for which no satisfactory solution could be found at that time. Then, in the early 1960s, a frame made of a steel alloy was manufactured. It was approximately 1" shorter than the standard racket and the head was round rather than the traditional oval shape. A second manufacturer then produced a competitive model which had similar design, and there are now several rackets on the market constructed of aluminum or other metal alloys.

It is claimed that, with the same stroke, a metal racket gives more power than a wooden one. The greater power is attributed to the greater flexibility of the metal which results in more of a whipping action. In addition, the metal frame is supposed to have greater durability. However, it is difficult to make any valid judgment of the efficacy of these rackets at this time, and their use is a matter of personal preference.

Strings

Two basic materials are currently being used to string tennis rackets: nylon and gut. Almost all rackets are strung with varying qualities of one of these. Each material has relative advantages and disadvantages.

Nylon string is most frequently used by beginning and intermediate players and in rackets furnished by schools. It is reasonably durable, gives good playing quality at a moderate cost, and is not susceptible to moisture, as is gut.

Although it is still possible to get an inexpensive monofilament nylon, it is not generally recommended. This string is a clear nylon with a slick playing surface. There is little friction as the ball contacts the strings and therefore less control than with other strings. The nylon recommended and more commonly used consists of strands woven to create a surface similar to gut. It is generally a white string with a red, green, blue, or black strand woven through it.

Gut is almost unanimously preferred and used by highly skilled players, who feel that it gives better playing quality. Although it is a durable string with normal usage, it does tend to absorb moisture. As moisture is absorbed the strings swell; if the moisture content becomes great enough, the strings will break. Gut, therefore, gives ideal playing quality but requires more care and is considerably more expensive.

Rackets can be purchased either factory strung or by the frame only. In the latter case, the buyer is then able to select the string preferred and to request a specific tension for the stringing. For the average player, 50 to 60 pounds is recommended.

TENNIS BALLS

Most beginning tennis players use tennis balls in varying states of wear, from those from which the outer covering is long gone and the ball is what tennis players term "light," to those which have lost nearly all bounce and when dropped from waist height barely rebound even a meager three or four inches. The ball used does affect a player's game and the learning of strokes. Therefore, it is important to give consideration to the tennis ball as well as to the racket.

Experienced tennis players will not use a ball after a portion of the white felt exterior is worn off. There is then less air resistance and a tendency for the ball to travel further with the same type of hit than would be the case with a new ball. When using a light ball, a player tends to change his strokes in an attempt to maintain or regain the control that existed when the ball was new, and this affects the quality of the game. In most tournaments, new balls are put into play every ninth or eleventh game.

Most tennis balls are made from rubber covered with a white material and inflated with compressed air. They are packed in airtight containers. Some balls are now being manufactured with a rubber center rather than one of compressed air; it is not necessary to package these balls in airtight containers. Although there are a variety of balls on the market, those used in tournament play must meet United States Lawn Tennis Association specifications.

CARE OF EQUIPMENT

If a player invests in a tennis racket, he will want to keep it in as good condition as possible. A racket generally requires little care and following a few simple rules will guarantee good service from it. A press is part of the equipment necessary for the care of a tennis racket. The press, a wooden frame which slips over the head of the racket and has screws at each of its four corners which can be uniformly tightened to exert an equal pressure over the head of the racket, helps keep the racket from warping. Many players feel there is no need for a press when the racket is being used regularly and when it is stored in a dry atmosphere between uses. It is undesirable to store a racket in a moist atmosphere for any length of time; if it is necessary to do so, a press should be used. Also, when a racket is to be stored for any length of time, regardless of the atmosphere, a press may prevent warping.

The strings in a tennis racket are made for hitting tennis balls, not other balls, rocks, or general debris. Since gut strings are susceptible to moisture, players should be particularly careful not to hit wet balls. Nylon strings are not as vulnerable to moisture, and whereas hitting a wet ball is not recommended, it would not be as harmful to nylon as it would to gut.

The strings in a tennis racket can at times be patched rather than completely replaced. After a period of use any string will begin to fray. If a player is contacting the ball in the center of the racket as he should, that area will wear first. It may be possible to have just the two or three center strings replaced. If this is to be done a player should not use a racket once a string breaks or is near breaking, for continued use will loosen adjacent strings.

DRESS

Tennis dress has come a long way since those early days of the game when fashion decreed that women wear skirts or dresses comprised of yards and yards of material which was to hang discreetly to the ankles. Similarly, men have been liberated from long trousers, traditional tennis attire for many years.

Today appropriate tennis dress consists, basically, of tennis shorts and a blouse (or any one of a variety of stylish tennis dresses) for women and a pair of tennis shorts and a shirt for men. This attire enables a player to be clean, neat, and well groomed and yet allows freedom of movement. Rubber-soled shoes should be worn by both men and women to prevent slipping, and to assist in the maintenance of the courts.

Tennis attire has traditionally been white, and where styles and lengths have changed, the characteristic color has remained the same throughout the years. Some tennis clubs will not allow members to play if they are not "appropriately" dressed, and there has been a common understanding that "appropriate" means white. There is a trend, though, toward the use of vivid contrasting colors added to a white costume, as well as toward the use of pastels in tennis dresses.

COURT SURFACES

The game we refer to today simply as "tennis" is actually "lawn tennis." When it was first brought to the United States it was played exclusively on grass. As the game increased in popularity and gradually moved from the east coast westward, other types of court surfaces began to be developed— essentially, it is believed, as a means of reducing the cost and time involved in the proper maintenance of a grass court. In addition, some surfaces are not as vulnerable to heavy rains as is grass, so it also became a matter of making courts more accessible in various types of weather. Whereas a grass court might not be playable for several days following a heavy rain, a concrete court could be ready within a few hours.

At the present time four basic court surfaces are used: (1) a grass surface, (2) a clay surface, (3) a concrete or cement surface, and (4) a wood surface. Each of these has its own characteristics, and a good player will adapt the style of his game to the characteristics of each. In addition, a variety of commercial surfaces are now being developed.

Grass. Although the ball has a relatively fast bounce on a grass court and at times may tend to skid, it bounces low and thereby fosters an aggressive game. Grass courts are used at Wimbledon and for most of the major tournaments in the eastern part of the United States as well as throughout Australia and England. For most play on grass, regular tennis shoes are used. However, if the grass is wet, players may be allowed to wear shoes with spikes to provide better traction.

Clay. The ball takes a slower bounce on clay courts than it does on grass. Hard serves and forcing volleys lose part of their effectiveness on clay because of the slower rebound, and the good player on a clay court is characteristically a retriever. Because of the slow rebound, the game is a slower one of long rallies. Players who adapt well to clay courts generally use long backswings in their strokes.

Concrete. The concrete court is a fast surface from which the rebound of the ball is both high and deep. The speed with which balls rebound from different concrete courts varies. One battery of courts may have a rough cement finish and a comparatively slow rebound while another battery will have a smoother finish and a faster rebound. The hardcourt game is characteristically an aggressive one in which players attempt to take advantage of a fast serve and a net game.

Wood. The fastest surface of all is the wood surface. Because of the speed with which the ball leaves the court, the player must use a very short backswing on the forehand and backhand drives. There is more accent on serving and volleying ability as the players attempt to move into position at the net.

Commerical surfaces. In recent years a number of commerically developed court surfaces have proven successful. These surfaces are combinations of various materials such as asphalt, cork, and plastic fibers. A synthetic grass-type carpeting that can be laid in 12" squares and replaced as an area wears has even been tried, with some success. Factors considered in the manufacture of court surfaces are the speed of the ball bounce, the height of the bounce, and the footing provided by the surface.

Indoor Courts

Another trend of recent years is the rapidly increasing popularity of indoor courts. There has been a tremendous increase in the number of indoor courts in this country within the last eight years, and the growing interest in tennis might be attributed to the increasing number of courts which allow for year-round play.

In the construction of indoor courts both fluorescent and mercury vapor lighting are being used, with either forced-air heating units or infrared lamps. A variety of court surfaces have been tried, ranging from the grass-like carpeting discussed previously to the traditional concrete to the newer composition courts. The initial cost of indoor courts is high, but maintenance costs are quite reasonable. More important, indoor courts allow year-round activity for all members of a community—housewives, businessmen, students, and youngsters—and therefore may well merit the investment.

The dimensions and markings on a tennis court remain the same with any surface. Fig. 2-2 shows a court with the names of the lines and areas indicated. This diagram should be studied until you can derive a concise mental image when reference is made to the baseline, the service line, or any other line or area on a court. Fig. 2-2 also includes the dimensions of the court, but as a reference source only. There is little purpose in memorizing the length of the various lines.

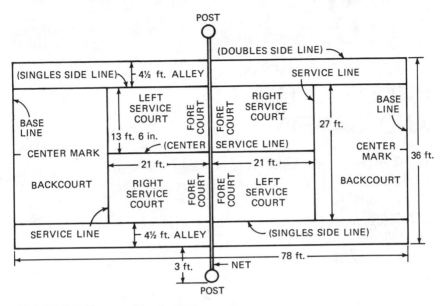

FIGURE 2-2. Diagram of tennis court

FROM THIS CHAPTER, YOU SHOULD HAVE LEARNED THAT:

A racket should be selected in relation to its weight, grip size, how it is strung, and how it feels to swing it.

Although most tournament competitors use gut, nylon string represents the best buy for the average player in terms of playing quality, cost, and durability.

Contemporary styles in tennis clothing enable players to be comfortable, have freedom of movement, and maintain a stylish appearance as well. White is the appropriate color for tennis.

The four most common court surfaces are grass, clay, concrete, and wood, although several commerical companies are developing synthetic surfaces.

Indoor courts seem to be a trend of the future since they allow for year-round play, as well as use from morning through late evening hours.

3

RULES, ETIQUETTE, AND SAFETY

The purpose of this chapter is to acquaint you with:
1. The fundamentals of scoring and other
   rules and regulations
2. Those practices considered common courtesy
   on the tennis court
3. Basic principles of safety

Tennis is one of the few games in which the rules and regulations are uniform throughout the world. National and international competition are played under the same rules, regulations, and code of conduct.

SCORING

The Game

Tennis uses what is perhaps the most unique scoring system of any of the popular sports played in the world today. There are four basic points in the game. The first point has a value of 15; the second point, 30; the third point, 40; and the fourth point has no numerical value but is simply, *game.* Thus, *15, 30, 40,* and *game* are the points which comprise the scoring system of tennis. Some players prefer to use *5* when scoring rather than *15,* and although *5* may be colloquially accepted, *15* is the technically correct terminology.

The term for a score of zero in tennis is *love.* Rather than "15 to nothing," or "15 to zero," it is "15-love" or "love-15," depending on whether the server or receiver won the first point. In tennis, *the server's score is always declared first.* If the receiver had won two points and the server had won no points, the score would be, "love-30."

Rather than saying "15 up" or "30 up" to denote an equal score, the term *all* is used. Therefore, if each player had won one point, the score would be "15 all"; if each had won two points, the score would be "30 all."

When each player has won three points the score is *deuce.* There is no numerical value, just the term. When the score reaches *deuce,* the game can no longer be won by a margin of one point; one player must win two consecutive points. The point following deuce is referred to as *advantage*; the player who has won the *advantage* is designated by "advantage server" or "advantage receiver." This score can also be designated by "advantage in," when it is the server's advantage, and "advantage out," when it is the receiver's advantage. These are the appropriate terms, but it is only fair to indicate that many tennis players find this terminology a little cumbersome and formal. They generally shorten *advantage* to *ad* and often designate the player who has won this point by simply "ad here" or "ad there."

If the score were *deuce* and the server won the next point, the score would be *advantage server.* If the receiver won the following point the score would revert to *deuce.* If the receiver won the next two points, the score would first be *advantage receiver* and then *game* for the receiver. Briefly, then, a player must win two consecutive points from a score of deuce to win a game.

The Set

The next unit of scoring in tennis is referred to as a *set.* A set is completed when one player wins six games and is at least two games ahead of an opponent. A player may win a *love set,* which would denote the opponent had won no games, or he may win a set by scores of 6-1, 6-2, 6-3, or 6-4, since each meets the two stipulations of (1) six games won and (2) being at least two games ahead. A score of 6-5 would not constitute a set since, although the first requirement has been met, the second has not. These players would continue to play until the set was complete, with scores such as 7-5, 8-6, 9-7, etc. In tournament competition such set scores occur frequently. Scores of 12-10 or 13-11 are less frequent, but occasionally sets will extend much further. In the 1969 Wimbledon Championships the score for one set was 24-22.

There should be a clear distinction between winning six games and playing six games. Two people could have a score of 4-2. Although one player is leading by two games and six games have been played, neither player has yet won six games, and therefore the set is incomplete.

Sudden Death

Because sets are frequently very long there have been occasional attempts to standardize their length by changing the manner in which they are scored. An innovation has recently been adopted by the U.S.L.T.A. on an experimental basis. It is referred to as the "sudden death" tie-breaker, and its use is permitted but is not mandatory. Thus either recreational players or tournament directors can decide whether to adhere to the traditional system of scoring the set or use the "sudden death" variation.

The "sudden death" tie-breaker approved by the U.S.L.T.A. goes into effect if a set becomes tied at 6 all. It is based on the winning of 5 out of 9 points, with each point having a numerical value of one. When players A and B have each won 6 games, they go into "sudden death." If A wins the first point the score is 1-0. If A wins the second point, it is 2-0. Play continues until one player wins 5 points. That player wins the set with the final score being 7-6. When playing "sudden death," it is not necessary to win by two games.

If a set becomes tied at 6 all and goes into "sudden death," the player who would normally serve the next game becomes the first server and serves two points—the first to the right court and the second to the left. The opponent serves the next two points also beginning with the right court. Players then change sides of the court and repeat the procedure. If neither player has won 5 points at this time, the second server serves the last point which completes the set.

If players A and B were playing doubles against C and D, A would serve the first two points and C the second two points; B would then serve the following two points, and D the next two. At any time a team scores 5 points, they win the set (7-6). If neither team has won after 8 points, player D would serve the 9th and deciding point. Teams alternate sides of the court after 4 points.

The Match

The third unit of scoring tennis players should be familiar with is that of a *match,* which consists of two out of three sets for women and three out of five sets for men. In tournament play, a two-out-of-three-sets match will often be used for men's competition; or two-out-of-three-sets matches will be played up to the semifinal or final rounds. At that point, the official three-of-five-sets match is played. Matches for both boys and girls who are 16 years of age or younger consist of two of three sets.

Match scores are reported with the score of the winner of the match given first. Thus, Smith may defeat Brown 6-3, 6-4. If Smith lost the second set but won the match, his score for each set would still be given first and thus would read 7-5, 2-6, 6-3. In the 1969 Wimbledon Tournament one men's singles match was won only after 112 games and five and one-half hours of play. The score was 22-24, 1-6, 16-14, 6-3, 9-7.

TOURNAMENT CLASSIFICATIONS

If a game of tennis is to be played by two people, it is referred to as a singles game; if it is to be played by four people, it is a game of doubles. Tournament competition is divided into men's singles and doubles divisions, women's singles and doubles divisions, and mixed couples (a man and a woman play against another man and woman).

In tournament play competitors are classified by age groupings and, in some areas, by skill groupings. Classification by age is accomplished by having divisions for those who are 12 years of age and under; 14 and under; 16 and under; and 18 and under. From the 18 and under division, players move to the men's and women's divisions and, ultimately, for those who maintain an interest in tournament competition, to a number of senior divisions for those who are over 35.

THE GAME

Spinning the Racket

Before players begin a game, it is necessary to determine who will serve first. In many sports, this is done by flipping a coin and calling *heads* or *tails.* On the tennis court, however, a coin may not be available; therefore players use the same principle but spin or toss the racket. In spinning the racket, you place the tip of the racket head on the ground, give it a spin, and allow the racket to fall. Players select some mark, usually a company trademark, which is on one side of the racket but not on the other and call for that side the same as they would for heads or tails. Some rackets have small decorative strings across the racket face near the tip and the throat. These strings are wound around the racket strings in such a manner that on one side of the racket face they present a smooth surface and on the other side they present a rough surface. In this case, players call *rough* or *smooth.*

The entire process of spinning the racket is to determine which player is to begin the game as the server and which sides of the court the players will begin upon. The winner of the toss may choose, or require his opponent to choose, (1) the right to be server or receiver, allowing the other player to choose the side of the court on which to begin, or (2) the side on which to begin, in which case the other player is allowed to choose whether he wants to serve or receive. Since the serve usually gives an advantage to a player, most players elect to serve first if they win the toss.

Alternating Courts

To equalize as nearly as possible such factors as sun, wind, or lighting, players periodically change sides of the court. The rule states that players will alternate sides after the first, the third, and every subsequent alternate game of a set. Therefore, if a player begins serving from the north side of a court, after the first game that player moves to the south side of the court. That player remains on the south court for two games and then alternates again. Since the change is made following the first game and every two games thereafter, players can easily remember when a change is to be made by totaling the number of games which have been played in a set. If the total is an even number, the players should remain as they are; if an odd number, the players should change sides.

Playing the Game

After an initial warm up, players begin a game by spinning the racket to determine who will begin serving and the side of the court each will begin upon and assuming positions for the first point. If player A is serving, he stands behind the base line approximately one step to the right of the center mark. The rules specify that the server can stand anywhere behind the base line between imaginary extensions of the center mark and the right singles side line for the first point. Strategically, though, it is wiser to remain near the center of the court. For doubles, it is suggested that the server move farther to the right. The serve for the first point of the game is always to the receiver's right service court. For the second point, the server stands behind the baseline one or two steps to the left of the center mark and serves diagonally across to the receiver's left service court. The serve continues to alternate between right and left service courts until a game is completed.

For a legal serve, the ball must be thrown into the air and hit before it touches the ground. It must travel across the net and bounce in the appropriate service court. The receiver is allowed to return the ball to anywhere within the boundary lines of his opponent's court. After the initial serve, the server may also hit the ball to anywhere within his opponent's court. The receiver must allow the ball to bounce on the serve; after the service return, however, the ball may be hit either before it bounces or after one bounce. It is never allowed to bounce more than once.

A player has two chances to hit the ball into the proper service court. If he fails with the first attempt, it is termed a *fault*. If he fails on both attempts, it is termed a *double fault* and the server loses that point.

Since two attempts are given for the serve, a server should always have two balls in his hand as he begins each point. This is not an official playing rule, but a courtesy. If the first serve is a fault, the second ball can immediately be served with neither the receiver nor the server having to wait while a second ball is retrieved. Having two balls to begin each point is a significant factor in saving time, energy, and often tempers.

The same server continues to serve throughout a game. At the end of the game the server becomes the receiver and the receiver becomes the server for the next game. The serve continues to alternate from player to player until a match is completed.

If playing doubles, one player serves through the first game, one of the opposing players serves through the second game, the partner of the first server serves through the third game, and the partner of the second server serves through the fourth game. This is then the established serving order and must be followed to the completion of a set.

COURT COURTESY

Around a tennis court you often hear the call, "A little help please." This call is a manner of asking players on another court for assistance in retrieving a ball, but it characterizes the courtesies generally practiced among tennis players. For example, if a ball rolls onto another court, rather than inter-rupting the play on that court to retrieve it, players wait until a point has ended. Then they can quickly retrieve the ball or ask one of the players on whose court it rolled to retrieve it. Players should never step onto another court or in any way distract players while play is in progress.

If you are requested to return a ball to players on an adjacent court, return it directly to them. It is little help when players have to chase a ball three or four courts in the opposite direction following a "helping" hit.

When entering tennis courts, it is courteous to wait until a point has been completed before entering the gate. If you are inside the gate, remain incon-spicuously near the fence until the point is completed. Once it is completed you can proceed quickly to your court.

As anyone who has spent much time around tennis tournaments realizes, catcalling, whistling, and booing are noticeably absent. Tennis has been characterized by a more restrained show of appreciation from spectators. Spectators clap in response to a good hit or a well-played point; they do not clap when a player misses the ball, hits it into the net, or serves a fault.

SAFETY RULES

Tennis does not involve much danger or hazard. However, a few basic safety rules should be followed. First, and probably most important, avoid jumping the net. A player jumping the net runs the risk of catching his toe in the top part of the net, which would throw him unceremoniously forward to the hard cement below. A player winning a match need not jump the net to congratulate his opponent but merely walk to the net and shake hands. Injuries from jumping the net range from severe loss of dignity to fractures of the arms and legs.

Avoid playing in the heat of the day without proper conditioning or adequate precautions. Players should gradually condition themselves to playing in hot weather and not attempt to become accustomed in one afternoon. Heat exhaustion and muscle cramps occasionally occur on hot days and in areas with high humidity, probably because of the loss of salt and water through normal perspiration. Players who play in high temperatures can prepare for the heat by taking salt tablets with adequate amounts of water before and during play.

Remove all balls from the court before play. Practice balls and those used in play become an obstacle if left on the court. Stepping on a ball could twist an ankle or cause other painful injury. Consequently, all balls should be removed before play begins.

Avoid playing on wet courts or smooth and slippery surfaces. These surfaces do not allow proper footing and present a hazard to both beginners and advanced players.

Always take time to warm up properly before beginning play. A long warm-up period increases the body temperature and allows the muscles to work faster and more efficiently. A warm up increases the proficiency of your shots and reduces the chance of pulling or straining a muscle.

AFTER COMPLETING THIS CHAPTER, YOU SHOULD:

Be able to play a tennis match using the proper scoring system, appropriate terminology, and adhering to tennis rules.

Use the method of spinning the racket to determine serve and starting position.

Change courts on alternate games and assume appropriate positions for serving and receiving.

Understand and follow the basic rules of safety and courtesy.

4

THE BASIC STROKES

This chapter will:
1. Provide a comparison of the various grips
   and an explanation of what is meant by the ready position
2. Analyze and give developmental activities for the forehand
   drive, the backhand drive, the serve, and the volley
3. Give several additional rules not discussed previously

The game of tennis provides little enjoyment until players develop sufficient control with their strokes to keep the ball in play. The basic objective for a beginning player, then, is the development of such control. Although repetition and practice are indispensable, an understanding of the mechanics of each stroke and its sequential development facilitates the learning process. Continual improvement in skills is based on an understanding and development of the fundamental mechanics of the strokes. It should be noted that all directions for stroking and positioning are given for right-handed players. Left-handed players should simply reverse these directions.

THE FOREHAND DRIVE

Grips

There are three ways in which the racket can be gripped for a forehand drive: a western grip, an eastern grip, and a continental grip. The eastern grip is the one preferred for the forehand drive and used by most tournament players today.

Eastern forehand. The eastern forehand grip is frequently referred to as the "handshake grip," since a player can easily as-

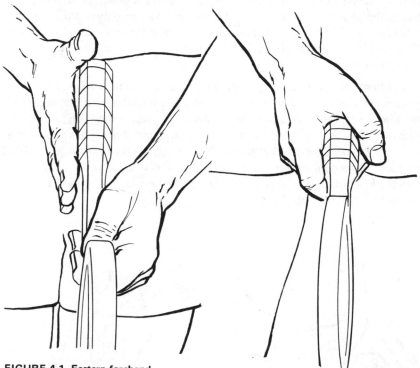

FIGURE 4-1. Eastern forehand

sume the grip by reaching forward as though to shake hands. As the hand meets the racket, the thumb should close over the top of the handle and the fingers, slightly spread, should close around the bottom. This grip places the "V" formed by the thumb and forefinger slightly to the right of the top plate of the racket handle, as shown in Fig. 4-1A.

The eastern forehand grip can also be assumed by allowing the throat of the racket to rest between the fingers and the thumb of the left hand with the racket head pointing directly forward. The right palm is placed flat against the racket face. Without turning the hand or racket face, the right hand is drawn down the strings to the handle. When the heel of the hand is resting against the butt of the racket handle, the fingers and thumb close firmly. The palm is against the side plate of the racket handle, as shown in Fig. 4-1B. At no time should the thumb or forefinger extend lengthwise on the handle, as this decreases the firmness of the grip.

Western. For a western forehand grip, the hand is turned approximately a quarter of a turn from the eastern position toward the player's right, so the palm is resting against the bottom plate of the racket handle. This movement places the face of the racket at a closed position, or downward angle, and facilitates the hitting of balls bouncing at or slightly above shoulder height. However, it makes the hitting of low balls awkward and, therefore, is not extensively used.

Continental. To assume a continental grip, the hand is turned from the eastern position one-eighth of a turn across the top of the handle, or toward the player's left side. This movement places the palm on the top plate of the racket handle. Hitting a forehand with the continental grip gives good racket position for low bouncing balls. For this reason, the continental grip is used by some European players whose games have developed on grass and clay courts, on which low bouncing balls are characteristic. This grip is, however, awkward for hitting high balls.

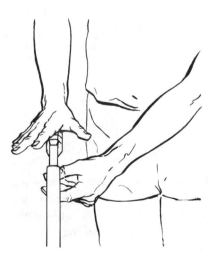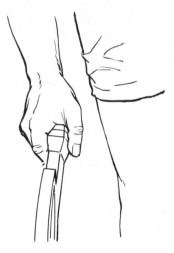

FIGURE 4-2. Eastern backhand

Backhand grip. To hit a ball which approaches on the player's left side, it is necessary to shift the hand on the racket from the eastern forehand grip to the eastern backhand grip by allowing the hand to rotate one-quarter of a turn toward the player's left. The hand and wrist rotate downward until the palm rests on the top plate of the racket handle. The thumb is angled diagonally downward and across the back of the grip. Fig. 4-2A shows this grip when looking at it from above and Fig. 4-2B shows the eastern backhand grip from the front.

The novice frequently attempts to develop a backhand stroke with the same grip used for the forehand. He fails to realize that, by changing to a backhand grip, he would gain better use of the muscles through the forearm. Backhand drives with a forehand grip are little more than "push" shots. The wrist can be held in a firm position while the player "pushes" the ball, but it cannot be held firm during a complete stroke. Therefore, power is never developed.

The eastern forehand grip and the eastern backhand grip are more advantageous than are others from the standpoint of ease of learning and the eventual development of power. The descriptions of the forehand and backhand drives assume the eastern forehand and backhand grips are being used.

Ready Position

The importance of the ready position cannot be overemphasized. First, it puts the individual in a position which facilitates movement in any direction, but more important, it is the position from which the strokes initiate. If the ready position is correct, chances are greater that the mechanics of the strokes and the grip change for the backhand will also be correct. In the early

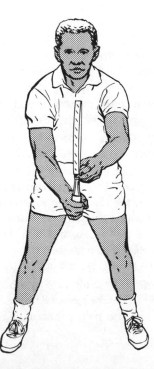

FIGURE 4-3. Ready position

stages of learning, moving from a ready position aids in coordination and in the eventual development of an easy rhythm.

A proper ready position can be assumed as follows:

1. Stand facing the net with the legs apart, knees slightly bent, and the weight evenly distributed and slightly forward. This stance allows you to move quickly in any direction.

2. Point the tip of the racket directly toward the net. Balance the racket at the throat on the first two or three fingers of the left hand with the thumb on top. Grip the racket handle firmly with the forehand grip with the right hand. The head of the racket should be slightly higher than the wrist.

3. Extend the racket arm forward. This position of the arm and use of the left hand at the throat of the racket can be seen in Fig. 4-3.

Developmental Activities

1. Hold the racket by the throat with the left hand and point the racket head directly forward. Grasp the handle with the eastern forehand grip. Check your grip by comparing it with Fig. 4-1. Next get the feel of the proper grip.

2. From a ready position, allow the fingers of the left hand to pull the throat of the racket to the left—the tip of the racket should be pointing toward the left sideline. Simultaneously, allow the right hand to rotate a quarter of a turn from the forehand to the backhand grip. Check the backhand grip with Fig. 4-2. Return to the ready position and repeat this movement until the shift is performed quickly, smoothly, and habitually. Establish a sense of feel for this motion.

3. With the forehand grip, bounce the ball in front of you with control. Perform as many bounces as possible in two-minute intervals. Keep a slight bend in the knees and bounce the ball about knee level. Keep the wrist and forearm firm to prevent slapping at the ball. This exercise will not only give you the feel of the forehand grip, but performing it for two-minute intervals should aid in strengthening the muscles of the forearm. It also provides practice in keeping the eyes on the ball; you should watch the ball contact the racket face with each hit.

4. With the forehand grip, hit the ball into the air and allow it to rebound off the racket face without contacting the ground. *Keep the wrist firm.* Practice for control beginning with low rebounds and gradually increasing until the ball is rebounding from three to four feet. Keep your eyes on the ball.

The Drive

The forehand drive is one of the most important offensive and defensive strokes and must be mastered with a maximum of power and control. For the beginning player, however, the ability to control the ball sufficiently to keep it in play is requisite to the enjoyment of the game and thus becomes the primary objective. The finished-form forehand drive requires a great deal of coordination, for as the stroking pattern increases in size and complexity, the problems of coordination and the chances for making error also increase. For this reason, the beginning player finds more immediate satisfaction in beginning with as simple a stroke as possible and progressing to the finished form.

Finished-form description. From a ready position, the wrist breaks directly in front of the body so the racket head is pointing to the right sideline (Fig. 4-4A). The arm continues to sweep the racket head straight back in a continuous movement to a point slightly beyond the right hip. With this action, the weight shifts onto the right foot and the movement of the racket and arm causes a rotation of the shoulders and hips to the right (Fig. 4-4B). The forward swing of the racket begins as the ball approaches. The player steps toward the net onto the left foot, swinging the racket forward. Simultaneously with the weight shift, the shoulders and hips rotate forward, bringing the racket forward to meet the ball. The racket contacts the ball in front of the forward foot as shown in Fig. 4-4C. The racket hits "through the ball," allowing the elbow to extend forward in the direction of the hit and maximizing the linear motion of the swing. The wrist remains firm throughout the stroke and especially through the hitting area. The racket continues in a slightly upward direction, finishing above shoulder level and pointing in the general direction of the left net post (Fig. 4-4D). The upper body has rotated forward with the forward swing and continues to the left with the follow through.

A rhythm should be developed which allows the stroking pattern to be continuous and smooth. If the ball approaches faster than usual, the total stroke has a faster movement, but all parts of it keep their basic relationship; no one movement is rushed. This rhythm comes with practice and the development of timing.

Now that we have looked at the complete stroke, attention can be given to the four distinct phases within the stroke—backswing, forward swing, contact point, and follow through. Although each phase is important to the total stroke, the contact point and follow through are the critical elements in achieving ball control and thus are considered first. The backswing and for-

FIGURE 4-4. Forehand drive. (A) Breaking of wrist; (B) completion of backswing; (C) contact point; (D) follow through.

ward swing are considered later since they are used to provide additional power through an increase in the size of the stroke.

Contact point. The first movement to occur in a forehand drive is a hyper-extension of the wrist, a "breaking" of the wrist. From a ready position, the wrist breaks directly in front of the body—that is, the racket head moves from a position pointing toward the net to a position pointing toward the right sideline, as shown in Fig. 4-4C. It should be emphasized that this movement occurs through the wrist. This breaking of the wrist creates a right angle between the racket and the forearm and provides the basic position for the racket in relation to the arm. This position of the wrist should be maintained throughout the stroke at the beginning levels. The arm should be away from the body and a slight bend maintained at the elbow. A step forward with the left foot (so the toes are pointing toward the right net post), which allows the left hip and shoulder to also come forward, places the player in the proper position to make contact with the ball.

At no time should the beginning player drop the racket head to hit a low ball or extend the arm completely to the side to hit a ball that is too far from him. Spatial adjustments should be made through the feet and knees.

Follow through. From the contact point the follow through consists of extending the arm forward and slightly upward in the direction of the hit until the elbow is completely extended and the arm is at shoulder level. As extension becomes complete, the momentum of the arm and racket pulls the right shoulder and hip forward, as was shown in Fig. 4-4D. The player should attempt to "hit through the ball," that is, to keep the ball on the string surface as long as possible from the contact point through the extension of the elbow, thereby directing it to the desired point.

Much of the power in the forehand drive comes from the extension of the elbow in the direction of the hit and from the weight shift. Control is achieved with the linear movement of the elbow extension while the ball is in contact with the strings.

For the beginning player it is essential for the wrist to remain solid at the contact point and throughout the follow through. If the wrist breaks before the arm is completely extended the stroke becomes a slap at the ball with a resultant loss of control. If the forearm and racket are allowed to roll over on the follow through so that the palm and racket face point downward, many balls will go into the net.

Backswing. The size of a player's backswing is related to his ability to control the ball. The larger the backswing, the more coordination is involved in hitting the ball and the greater the chances for error. Thus, for a player just learning the strokes, the racket should be taken back five to six inches from the contact point. When the ball can be controlled, the length of the backswing can be increased. If control is lost, the backswing can be shortened. The backswing taken by advanced players varies with such factors as the court surface, height of the ball, and their ability to control the ball.

The backswing begins from a ready position. As his opponent hits the ball, the player's wrist *breaks,* signaling the beginning of his backswing. The racket head continues back with the shoulders and hips following. With this movement, the weight shifts to the rear foot. This position is shown in Fig. 4-4. Note the maintenance of the wrist position and the slight bend in the elbow.

Forward swing. As the ball approaches, the forward swing begins. The racket begins moving forward *on a level with the approaching ball.* The player steps forward onto the left foot as the racket swings forward. The racket meets the ball at the contact point in front of the forward foot. The elbow straightens out, hitting "through" the ball, and the racket, traveling in a slightly upward path, finishes just above shoulder level.

Developmental Activities

1. Assume a contact position. Check yourself or, if working in partners, check one another on the following points:

 a. The left foot should be forward.

 b. The wrist is *broken*, creating a right angle between the forearm and the racket. The upper arm is away from the body, but there is a slight bend in the elbow.

 c. The racket head is at, or slightly above, wrist level; the racket face is perpendicular to the ground.

 d. The racket is at least even with, and preferably in front of, the forward foot.

2. Work in pairs. Have one player (the hitter) assume the contact position while the other (the thrower) throws the ball. The thrower stands approximately six feet from the hitter and throws the ball with an easy underhand motion. It can be thrown first with no bounce so that it hits in the center of the racket face, or, if preferred, it can be thrown so that it will bounce once and rebound to a position near the racket face. At this point, spatial adjustments for the hitter should be minimized so he can concentrate on maintaining the correct contact position; therefore, the ball thrower must throw the ball as accurately as possible so the hitter can simply "bump" the ball back. The contact position should be maintained with no release of the wrist. You should acquire the ability to bump 15 balls directly back to the thrower with

no loss of control. When this can be done routinely, you are ready to add the next phase of the stroke.

3. Again, you should work in pairs, using a hitter in the contact position and a ball thrower six feet away. The ball should be thrown with an underhand motion so that it will bounce once and rebound as near the hitter's racket face as possible. The hitter should meet the ball at the contact point, straighten his arm in the direction of the hit, and direct the ball to the thrower. The wrist and forearm must remain firm throughout the motion. When you can hit a minimum of 12 out of 15 balls in this manner without loss of control, you are ready to progress to the next task.

4. At this point, the hitter should begin to make spatial adjustments. If the ball is high, the arm can be raised; but the relationship with the elbow, wrist, and racket must be maintained. If the ball is low, the adjustment should be made by bending the knees. If the ball is slightly to the hitter's right, he should step toward the ball enough to contact it at the proper position. If the ball is too close, the hitter can step away sufficiently to maintain the proper hitting position.

Continuing to work in pairs, the thrower should begin throwing balls for which the hitter must make these minor spatial adjustments. As you (the hitter) begin to move around, you should be able to maintain the same amount of control with the ball returns as you had from a stationary position. Therefore, when you can return 12 out of 15 balls from the proper hitting position directly to the thrower, you are ready to add some backswing to your stroke.

5. This time the hitter begins from a ready position. The ball thrower, from a distance of approximately 15 feet, uses an underhand throw so that the ball rebounds into hitting position. The hitter begins with a minimal backswing of five to six inches and gradually increases the backswing to the limits of his ability to control the ball. Again, 12 of 15 balls should be returned to the thrower with control. The thrower should attempt to correct the hitter if necessary, on the following points:

a. Is each stroke started from a ready position?

b. Does the wrist set at the beginning of each stroke so that the head of the racket leads on the backswing?

c. Is the backswing and forward swing smooth? Do they allow contact with the ball to be made in front of the forward foot with the elbow slightly bent and the racket head at or slightly above the wrist?

d. Do the elbow and racket extend forward as a unit as the ball is contacted, directing it to the desired spot?

6. As partners, stand on opposite sides of the net at your respective service lines and attempt to keep the ball in play using the forehand stroke with a modified backswing. As control is achieved, move back slightly and increase the size of the backswing. Gradually move to the back of the court and progress to the finished form. Always allow your progress to be determined by your ability to control the ball.

7. *Backboard Practice.* The backboard can be an excellent asset to the development of tennis skill when used correctly. It should not be used by the beginning player to see how forcefully the ball can be hit. The player developing strokes to achieve ball control should use the board by standing six to eight feet from it. The racket should be in a position to begin a forward swing as the ball is dropped in front of the forward foot. The player, using a modified backswing, bumps the ball into the backboard. The instant it rebounds the racket should be moving forward to contact it again. Players should attempt to develop control and rhythm. When the ball can be controlled for 15 consecutive hits, the player can move back an additional five feet. As control is achieved, the size of the backswing and the distance from the board can be increased until the player is using a finished-form forehand drive.

THE BACKHAND DRIVE

The backhand drive is as fundamental to the game as the forehand drive and should be developed to provide the player with both power and control. The backhand employs a natural swinging pattern and in many respects is easier to hit than the forehand. The stroke should be one continuous, smooth, and rhythmical motion. An understanding of the components of the stroke should help the player achieve proficiency; consequently the following pages describe the backswing, forward swing, contact point, and follow through.

Backswing

The backswing begins from a ready position. As your opponent hits the ball to your left side, the fingers of the left hand immediately pull the throat of the racket to the contact point in front of the body. Simultaneously, the right hand gripping the racket rotates a quarter of a turn to the left for the backhand grip. This action will be referred to as *breaking* the wrist to the contact point and is the first movement that occurs with the stroke (see Fig. 4-5A). The left hand continues to pull the arm and racket straight back about

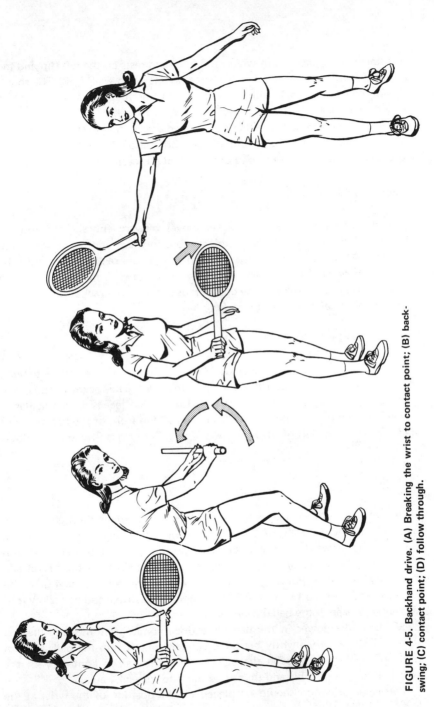

FIGURE 4-5. Backhand drive. (A) Breaking the wrist to contact point; (B) backswing; (C) contact point; (D) follow through.

waist height to a position in which the left hand rests on the left hip and the racket head is perpendicular to the fence, as shown in Fig. 4-5B. The shoulders and hips rotate back with the racket until the player is sideways to the net with the weight on the back foot.

The beginning student should be cautioned against taking too large a backswing as it necessitates greater timing and coordination. Many teachers recommend the backswing be shortened until control has been mastered.

Forward Swing

As the ball approaches, the racket moves forward and slightly upward. Simultaneously, the shoulders and hips rotate forward, and the weight gradually shifts from the rear to the forward foot as the racket approaches the ball at the contact point. There is no hesitation between the backswing and forward swing; the stroke is one continuous motion. The racket should move forward *on a level with the approaching ball.*

Contact Point

At the point of contact the body is in a position with the side to the net, the right foot forward, and the knees slightly bent. The racket head is even with or slightly higher than the wrist, and the racket face is perpendicular to the court. The ball should be met from 6 to 10" in front of the forward foot and slightly to the left of the body (Fig. 4-5C). The grip is firm and the elbow is slightly bent.

Follow Through

As contact with the ball is made, the elbow straightens through the ball, guiding it in the direction of the hit. The arm and racket continue to extend forward and upward to a shoulder-high position. The shoulders and hips simultaneously rotate until the player is facing the net with the racket and arm fully extended, pointing to the right side of the court (Fig. 4-5D). The beginner should keep his wrist firm throughout the stroke and not allow it to straighten or slap at the ball during the hit.

Much of the power in the backhand drive comes from meeting the ball with the elbow very slightly bent and straightening it into the ball. Control develops by hitting through the ball, keeping the ball in contact with the strings as long as possible and thus directing it to a specific area.

Particular attention should be placed on the position of the wrist at the contact point and throughout the follow through. If the wrist breaks, straightens out, or rolls over during the hit, control is lost. It is therefore recommended that the beginner hold the wrist firm throughout the entire stroke.

Developmental Activities

1. From a ready position allow the fingers of the left hand to pull the throat of the racket to the left; allow the wrist to break to the contact point. Return to the ready position and repeat this movement several times. Assume a contact position. Check yourself, or, if working in partners, check one another to see if:

a. The wrist is *broken*, creating an angle between the forearm and the hand, and the player has a backhand grip.

b. The racket is in front of the forward foot; the racket head is level with, or slightly above, the wrist. The racket face is perpendicular to the court.

c. The right foot is forward.

2. Work in pairs. Have one player assume the contact position while the other throws the ball just as he did for the forehand drive practice. The ball hitter should concentrate on maintaining the contact position and simply bump the ball to the thrower. The thrower must get the ball as near to the contact position as possible. You should acquire the ability to bump 15 consecutive balls directly back to the thrower with no loss of control.

3. The hitter again assumes a contact position. The ball is thrown from a distance of six feet with an easy underhand motion so it will bounce once and rebound as near the racket face as possible. The hitter should meet the ball at the contact point and straighten his arm into the ball in the direction of the hit, returning the ball to the thrower. The player is essentially using a contact position and follow through. The wrist and forearm remain firm. When you can hit a minimum of 12 out of 15 balls in this manner without loss of control, you are ready to progress to the next step.

4. The ball can now be thrown so the hitter has to make minor spatial adjustments. The spatial adjustments are made with the feet and knees; the same contact position is maintained. The hitter uses a very small backswing and emphasizes the contact position and follow through. When you can return a minimum of 12 out of 15 balls to the hitter with control you are ready to continue.

5. The hitter begins from a ready position. The ball thrower moves to a

distance of approximately 15' from the hitter and continues to use an under-hand throw so that the ball rebounds into hitting position. The hitter uses a minimal backswing of five to six inches and gradually increases the backswing as his ability to control the ball increases. The thrower should attempt to correct the hitter on the following points if necessary:

a. Does the wrist break to the contact point with a simultaneous grip change?

b. Is racket pulled back at waist level with elbow slightly bent? Are shoulders and hips sideways to the net?

c. Does the racket sweep forward and upward to contact the ball in front of the forward foot and slightly to the left of the body?

d. Does the follow through extend through the ball in the direction of the hit?

e. Do the shoulders and hips rotate forward with the weight shift and follow through?

6. Partners stand on opposite sides of the net at their respective service lines and attempt to keep the ball in play using the backhand stroke with a modified backswing. As control is achieved, players gradually move toward the baseline and increase the size of the backswing. Progress to the finished-form backhand drive, but allow progress to be determined by your ability to control the ball.

7. *Backboard Practice.* The backboard can be a useful practice device for the backhand drive as well as for the forehand drive if used properly. Employ the same technique as described for the forehand. Remember to break the wrist before dropping the ball and attempt to establish a rhythm with the hits. Begin at a distance of from six to eight feet from the board and bump the ball. Gradually move back and increase the backswing as control is acquired.

THE SERVE

The serve is probably the most important single stroke in the game. With a proper delivery a player can win outright many points in the games in which he serves. To develop a powerful and accurate serve a player must have a basic understanding of the elements comprising the serve and be willing to devote hours of practice to the development of his serve. The beginner must concentrate on ball control and not attempt to develop power until his service motion is established and a degree of consistency is attained.

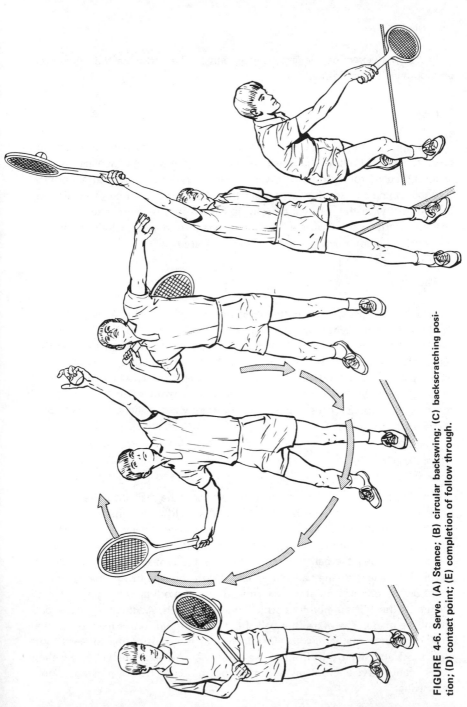

FIGURE 4-6. Serve. (A) Stance; (B) circular backswing; (C) backscratching position; (D) contact point; (E) completion of follow through.

Let us now examine the grip, stance, and stroke and trace the sequential development to the finished form.

Grip

The continental grip is widely used as a service grip by most tournament players. This grip allows the server flexibility in the choice of services as well as the potential for maximum power through wrist snap at the contact point.

A beginning student, however, may find it extremely difficult to maintain ball control with the continental grip. It is therefore recommended that the beginner learn to serve with an eastern forehand grip, eventually changing to the continental after consistency has been mastered.

The Stance

Most players prefer to stand in a position sideways to the net with the toe of the left foot slightly angled toward the net post and just behind the baseline. The feet should be comfortably spread apart with the weight on the rear foot. The racket is held in front of the body and pointing in the direction of the receiver. The elbow of the right arm is slightly bent. The ball is held in the fingers of the left hand. The left hand is in front of the body, lightly touching the strings of the racket, and the right wrist is slightly cocked. (See Fig. 4-6A.)

The Ball Throw

The objective of the ball throw is to place the ball into the air with complete accuracy and consistency. The ball should rest in the fingers of the left hand about waist high. As the right arm moves downward to start the service backswing, the left arm drops down slightly and then slowly extends upward, releasing the ball from the fingers as the arm extends to maximum reach. The height of the ball throw varies with the size of different players. The correct contact point is determined by extending the right arm and racket to the highest point to which you can reach. At this height contact should be made. Therefore, the ball should be thrown to this height and to a position approximately six to eight inches to the right of the forward foot (left foot) and slightly in front of the base line. An accurate ball throw eliminates many service problems and must be mastered before moving to the backswing.

Backswing

The backswing begins from the service stance position, in which the racket is in front of the body and the elbow is slightly bent and pointing in the direction in which you are about to serve. The right arm and racket begin to move straight down in a semicircular motion as the left arm extends upward to release the ball (Fig. 4-6B). The arm straightens as the racket passes the right leg and moves away from the body. As the arm approaches shoulder level, the elbow begins to bend until both arm and racket are pointing downward behind the body in a "back-scratching" position (Fig. 4-6C). The right shoulder has rotated away from the net, and the weight is on the rear leg as the ball approaches its full height.

The Hit

From the back-scratching position, the right arm extends upward and forward, with the wrist and racket head slightly trailing. The weight begins to shift forward and the right shoulder rotates toward the net as the arm and elbow fully extend (Fig. 4-6D). The wrist snaps the head of the racket through the ball at the point of contact. This point is a little to the right of the body and about 8 to 12" in front of the base line.

Follow Through

The right arm and racket are in a straight line at the contact point. The wrist snaps the racket head through the ball and the arm follows in the direction of the ball's flight. The arm and racket sweep through the ball and across the left side of the body (Fig. 4-6E). The right foot moves forward across the base line and steps into the court. The step with the right foot not only aids in balance but also facilitates the advanced player's movement toward the net.

Developmental Activities

The full service stroke requires timing and coordination beyond the capabilities of most beginning students. Consequently, it is often necessary to alter the teaching procedure to better correspond to the ability of the students. A method preferred by many teachers is to divide the service motion into two distinct parts: the ball throw-backswing and the hit-follow through. Each of these parts can be mastered independently and later combined into a full stroke. Listed below is the developmental sequence preferred.

1. *Ball Throw and Backswing.* From the service stance position, the service motion begins as the racket starts down and the left arm moves up to throw the ball. As the ball is released, the right arm and racket move down the back to a back-scratching position. Stop the motion at this point; allow the ball to bounce to check the accuracy of the ball throw. The ball should land slightly to the right of the body about eight to 12 inches in front of the baseline. A second ball can be placed on the court at this position to serve as a target. This exercise should be performed until the motion is accurate, smooth, and rhythmical, and the ball throw is both accurate and consistent.

2. *Hit and Follow Through.* The racket and arm should be placed behind the back in the back-scratching position. After the racket is in place, the ball is thrown with the left hand. The right arm and racket move upward and forward to meet the ball. At the contact point, the arm and racket are fully extended. The racket head moves through the ball and guides it out and over the net. The follow through ends on the left side of the body.

The hitting of the ball should be practiced until the beginner can get 80 percent of his serves into the proper court. The size of the backswing can be shortened or lengthened according to the ability of the student to control the ball.

3. *Full stroke.* After both the preceding developmental exercises have been mastered, the student is ready to combine the ball throw, hit, and follow through into a complete service motion. The motion should be continuous, smooth, and rhythmical. Major emphasis should be placed on consistency; speed and power can be developed after control and consistency have been mastered.

4. *Summary.* Work in partners and check one another on the following points:

a. Does player have proper service grip?

b. Are feet apart for balance with left shoulder pointing toward the court to which the ball will be served?

c. Are racket and balls held slightly above waist level with the end of the racket pointing toward the court to which the ball will be served?

d. Are two balls held in the fingers of the left hand with the palm facing upward?

e. Is the ball throw six to eight inches to the right of the left foot and slightly in front of the baseline?

f. Does the elbow bend on the backswing until the racket is in a back-scratching position?

g. Is the arm fully extended at the point of contact with the ball?

h. Is the follow through a natural motion with the shoulders rotating to the left?

THE VOLLEY

The volley (any ball hit in the air before it bounces) is basic to the game of tennis and should be developed by every player at least to the point where that player can feel comfortable in a position close to the net. In men's singles competition the volley is part of what has become known as the "Big Game," in which the server uses the hard, fast serve and follows it to the net where he can volley the return. The speed of the serve places the receiver on the defensive, and if the server has been able to establish position at the net, he can keep the receiver on the defensive with sharp volleys. The Big Game, therefore, is characteristically a game of serves and volleys.

Because of differences between men and women in strength and speed, the Big Game is essentially a man's game. Top women competitors do use net play more frequently now than in the early years of tennis, but their games are based to a greater extent on ground strokes. However, the volley is an offensive tool for singles play and is absolutely essential to good doubles play. Therefore, the volley is a basic stroke which should be developed by an aspiring tennis player—man or woman.

The Grip

To hit a volley, the traditional grip used has been a forehand grip for a forehand volley and a backhand grip for a backhand volley. However, since the advent of the Big Game, many tournament players have adopted the continental grip for both forehand and backhand volleys. The obvious advantage of a single grip is that it requires less time to move from forehand to backhand position, which enables a player to cover the net more adequately. The advantage of the continental grip is that it provides greater power on the backhand volley than could be achieved with a forehand grip. It also facilitates hitting the volley with the slight underspin necessary for control. It does, however, require greater wrist strength on the forehand volley than is required by an eastern forehand grip.

In deciding whether to adopt a single grip or change from forehand to backhand grips, a player should consider his goal. If he is aiming to develop into a serious tournament competitor, it is recommended that he learn to volley using the continental grip. If he is less competitively oriented and is thinking of tennis in a strictly recreational sense, he may derive more immediate satisfaction from using a forehand grip for the forehand volley and changing to a backhand grip for a backhand volley.

Stance and Court Position

A player should position himself as close to the net when volleying as he can play and still defend against the lob. Most tournament players play six to eight feet from the net and then move forward to meet the ball as soon as they anticipate its direction. A player who volleys the ball in a position close to the net has more accurate placement and commits fewer errors than one who attempts to volley from midcourt for the following reasons: (1) being close to the net provides the volleyer much greater angles at which to place the ball; (2) it is easier to cover or "cut off" the short-angled passing shot from the opponent; (3) the net represents less of a barrier, as the ball can be contacted before it drops below the top of the net; and (4) the ball, after it is volleyed, travels a shorter distance and is in the air a shorter time which allows an opponent less time to prepare for a return.

The stance for the volley is similar to the stance for the ready position, about the only difference being that the racket head is carried a little higher. The legs are comfortably apart, knees slightly bent, and weight on the balls of the feet. From this position a player can move quickly in any direction.

The Hit

A fundamental difference between the volley and any other stroke is that, *for a beginner,* there is practically no backswing and little follow through. It involves shifting from the ready position to the point of contact with as little motion as possible, and thus in as little time as possible. The swing becomes a controlled punch at the ball, and the follow through is the natural recoil of the racket as the ball strikes it.

As the ball approaches the right side of the body, the wrist breaks, which allows the racket head to move forward and upward. The player simultaneously steps forward with the *left* foot, transferring his weight *forward* to

FIGURE 4-7. Contact point for fore-hand volley

meet the ball. The point of contact is in front of the left foot. The racket face is slightly open to allow a slight backspin to be imparted to the ball for control. This contact position is shown in Fig. 4-7.

If the ball approaches the left side, the wrist breaks and pulls the racket from the ready position to the contact position as the player steps *forward* with his *right* foot, transferring his weight forward to meet the ball.

FIGURE 4-8. Contact point for back-hand volley

At the point of contact for either a forehand or backhand volley, the wrist remains firm. Power is generated by the forward step and by a forward punch with a solid wrist and forearm. The wrist should never be allowed to snap or flip forward.

For a ball that drops below the net, the contact position is lowered by bending the knees to the level at which the ball will be hit. The racket face must then be opened sufficiently to allow a rebound of sufficient height to clear the net. This contact position for low volleys is shown in Fig. 4-8.

Developmental Activities

To develop an adequate volley it is necessary to learn the proper footwork and feel the volley as a short punch without a large backswing or follow through.

1. Stand six feet from the net in a ready position. Have partner throw the ball to the forehand side with no bounce. Step forward as the wrist breaks to meet the ball at the point of contact. There is a slight forward movement of racket and forearm and the wrist is held firm as the ball contacts the racket. Return to the ready position following each hit. Each hit should be made with a step toward the net on the left foot.

2. Repeat exercise to the backhand side. Check to see that the step forward is taken on the right foot. There should be little shoulder rotation.

3. Alternate ball throw to forehand and backhand side. Continue until hitter has feeling for the mechanics involved and can consistently and rhythmically move in either direction to make contact. Some ball throws should be low requiring the hitter to adjust the contact position by bending the knees.

4. Two players stand on opposite sides of the net, approximately six feet from the net, and attempt to volley the ball between them. This provides practice in adjusting both body and racket position quickly, in watching the ball, and in contacting the ball with control. This particular exercise has no value if either player volleys the ball hard or allows the racket head to come forward on the hit with a resultant loss of control. The objective is to achieve controlled volleys between two players.

5. One player positions himself two to three feet behind the service line with the second player in a volleying position across the net. The first player hits the ball to the net player with a forehand drive. The net player volleys

the ball back to the hitter. Repeat several times to the forehand, to the backhand, and then alternate.

6. As the volleyer becomes adept at moving into position and achieving a solid contact, the hitter can gradually move toward the baseline and attempt to keep the ball in play by baseline drives and volleys.

ADDITIONAL RULES

Although reference has been made to the basic rules of tennis, there are a few additional rules with which players should be familiar. No attempt has been made to list all the rules of the game, and for further clarification or for the complete rules of tennis, the reader is referred to *The Official United States Lawn Tennis Association Yearbook.*

The Net

The rules specify that the net shall be three feet in height at the center and 3'6'' at the net posts. Players can judge whether the net is the proper height at the center of the court by placing the end of one racket on the ground so it is standing vertically and setting a second racket on the end of the first horizontally. If minor changes are needed they can be made by adjusting the tension of the center strap or the net cord.

Serving

Although the position assumed by the server has been discussed, there are additional rules relating to positioning and the service motion. For example, the server is not allowed to change his position by walking or running during the serve. His feet may not touch the base line or the court inside the base line from the beginning of the service motion until the racket has contacted the ball. Failure to obey these rules constitutes a fault. Note, however, that this ruling does not preclude the possibility of the foot swinging over the base line, as long as contact with the ground is not made until the racket has contacted the ball.

For the first point of a game, the service is from the right of the center mark diagonally across the net into the receiver's right service court; for the second point it is from the left of the center mark to the receiver's left service court. The service alternates in this manner throughout a game.

If it is discovered during the game that the serve has been to the wrong court, the points already completed stand. The server then immediately corrects his position so that subsequent serves are directed to the correct court.

The problem of serving the ball to the correct court may be alleviated if players think of the receiver's right-hand service court as the *even* court and the receiver's left-hand service court as the *odd* court. If an even number of points has been played in a game, the subsequent serve will be to the receiver's right court; if an odd number of points has been played in the game, the subsequent serve would be to the receiver's left court. Deuce is an even score, so the server would deliver the next ball to the receiver's right court; if the score were advantage (for either player), the next serve would be directed to the receiver's left court.

If a server throws the ball into the air to serve it and then decides not to hit it, the action is not considered a fault. Occasionally the server gets a bad ball throw or the wind carries the ball out of position. If this occurs, it is better to catch the ball and throw it again rather than attempt to serve. If, however, the server throws the ball into the air, strikes at it, and misses the ball entirely, it is considered an attempt to serve and is ruled a fault.

The server must wait until the receiver is ready before serving the ball. If the receiver makes an attempt to return the served ball, he is considered to have been ready. If he is not ready, he should make no attempt to hit the ball and immediately signify that he was not ready.

Let Ball

Any ball that does not count and is played over is referred to as a *let*. A served ball that touches the net and yet goes into the proper service court is a let. When this occurs, the ball is re-served. If a ball which has been served and is in play touches the net and goes into the proper court, it remains in play.

If a player is hindered when making a stroke by something over which he had no control, the rules stipulate that a *let* be called and the point be replayed. This call could occur if a spectator interfered with a player or if an object, such as another ball, rolled onto a court while a point was in progress.

Playing the Ball

A ball striking a boundary line is legal. A ball is not considered out of bounds until it touches the ground, a permanent fixture, or any other object *outside* of the boundary lines. Therefore, if a player stepped outside the court and caught a ball which had not bounced and which was obviously going to be out of bounds, he would be in violation of the rules and would lose the point. If a player is standing out of bounds and volleys a ball, that ball remains in play if the return falls within the boundaries of his opponent's court; if he volleys it into the net, he loses the point.

One of the more interesting rules of tennis provides that, if a player is hit with a ball which is in play, the player who has been hit not only loses his dignity but also the point. This is true regardless of whether the player hit was standing in or out of the court boundaries.

Net Play

It is illegal for a player to touch the net or to allow his racket or clothing to touch or even brush against the net while the ball is in play. Nor may a player reach across the net to hit the ball. If a player contacts the ball on his side of the net, it is legal for the racket and even the arm to cross the net on the follow through, providing the player does not contact the net with his body, nor racket, or clothing.

Doubles Play

The rules and scoring of tennis for doubles are the same as those for singles. An additional 4½' are added to each side of the court making it wider and constitute the doubles sidelines. It should be noted, though, that the service court remains exactly the same in doubles as in singles. A served ball landing in the alley in singles or doubles is a fault.

In doubles the server is allowed to position himself anywhere between the center mark and the doubles sideline.

One member of a doubles team receives serves in the right service court and the other member receives serves in the left service court. When the ball is served to the right court, the player receiving in that court must return or attempt to return the ball. The other player is not allowed to return the serve. Once a player begins receiving serves in the right service court, that player continues to receive serves to the right court throughout the set. At no time during the set is it legal for that player to receive serves to the left court; this rule seems to be the most frequently misunderstood and violated by beginning players.

If one player on a doubles team strikes at a ball and misses it completely, his partner could legally return, or attempt to return, the ball. If the ball contacts the racket of one player, however, his partner could not legally return it.

AFTER READING THIS CHAPTER, YOU SHOULD KNOW:

The differences among the various grips and which one to assume for a given stroke.

How to assume the ready position and its importance to quick movement.

The fundamentals and finished form of the forehand drive, the backhand drive, the serve and the volley.

PART

II

One Step
Further

5

HISTORICAL DEVELOPMENT AND CONTEMPORARY TRENDS

This chapter should provide some insight into:
1. The highlights of the early history
and development of tennis
2. Significant landmarks in the history of the game
since its arrival in the United States
3. Breaks with tradition in the tennis realm

HISTORICAL HIGHLIGHTS

Although there is evidence of games which bore some resemblance to the modern game of tennis having been played over 500 years before the Christian era, the forerunner of our modern game achieved popularity in France and subsequently in England in the fifteenth and sixteenth centuries. The game, very popular with kings and monarchs, soon became known as the "sport of kings." It has even been reported that this forerunner of tennis was responsible for the death of King Louis X of France, in that he was alleged to have contracted a chill following a particularly vigorous game (Nikolic, 1970)!

It seems to be a law of nature that what royalty and the rich have, the less affluent aspire to, and although the monarchs of the courts tried, they had a difficult time keeping the game from the knights, soldiers, and "common people." Kings Edward III and Richard II outlawed tennis because their soldiers and knights, instead of practicing the arts of warfare, seemed to dally all their time away batting a ball over a rope. However, by the nineteenth century, tennis began to spread beyond aristocratic circles and became a popular game among the peoples of France and England.

As the game progressed and changed, so too did the equipment. At one time the ball was simply a roll of fabric and string. Next it became a skin filled with the long hair of women. It is left to your discretion to determine the significance of the belief that a ball filled with blond hair gave more bounce than one filled with dark hair (Nikolic, 1970)!

The ball was originally batted back and forth over a rope with only the hand. A glove was then added, presumably as a protective covering. We might further surmise that a wooden paddle and ultimately the racket we know today developed as a result of some sore palms.

The tennis court also changed. The original court was shaped like an hourglass—narrower at the net than at the baseline. In seventeenth century England, the net was five feet high at the side posts and three feet at the center of the court. It is felt the game might have resembled volleyball played with a racket.

Whereas the early game was played on an indoor court, its descendant became known as "tennis-on-the-lawn," and then, "lawn tennis." It is interesting to note, too, that the game we play today and refer to simply as tennis is literally the game of lawn tennis—whether it is being played on lawn, cement, or any of the several surfaces available.

Major Walter C. Wingfield, a British Army officer, is credited with taking the basic principles of the indoor game and fitting them to outdoor play. The game he devised was a success; but the name he chose for it—*Sphairistike*—was both difficult to pronounce and to remember. The game succeeded, but the name failed (Buchanan, 1951).

The game became a popular pastime of the British Army and soon reached the military post at Bermuda. Mary Outerbridge, an American then visiting Bermuda, was introduced to the game, became interested, and on her return home to Staten Island in 1874, brought both the necessary equipment and enthusiasm to initiate the game in this country. In the next few years, interest and participation increased remarkably, and by 1880 the first important tournament was held at the Staten Island Club (Buchanan, 1951).

During those early years the rules and equipment of the game varied greatly. Balls were of different sizes, rackets were of different shapes, and the height of the net varied as well as the court dimensions. In 1881 the United States Lawn Tennis Association (USLTA) was formed, and soon the rules and equipment became standardized.

CONTEMPORARY TRENDS

The USLTA is still the governing body of amateur tennis in the United States and is a member of the International Lawn Tennis Federation. The USLTA functions through 16 sectional organizations in assuming responsibilities such as sanctioning tournaments, publishing and interpreting the official rules of the game, and establishing national and sectional rankings for players. It is also the agency which sponsors our teams for international competition, including the United States Davis, Wightman, and Federation Cup Matches.

In 1900, Dwight F. Davis instigated international team matches for men and contributed a large sterling silver bowl, which became known as the "Davis Cup," for the symbol of the team championship. Soon after, Hazel H. Wightman conceived of a similar competitive event for women of the United States and England, and this team event became known as the Wightman Cup Matches. It was not until 1963 that the ILTF created the Ladies International Team Competition, or what are known as the Federation Cup Matches, to provide international team competition for women in much the same manner as the Davis Cup competition for men. These matches allow countries which are members of the ILTF to participate with one another on a team basis.

Many countries now sponsor national tournaments. The "grand slam" of tennis consists of winning the United States, Australian, French, and Wimbledon (English) national tournaments in one season. It represents the epitome of individual tennis supremacy and has been achieved only four times in the history of the game. Don Budge, an American, was the first to score the grand slam; next was Maureen Connolly who, when she won, was less than 20 years of age; and more recently Rod Laver, an Australian, was able to garner the four required wins. In 1969 Rod Laver made an unprecedented second grand slam.

A particularly significant factor in the contemporary development of tennis was the first tournament to allow open competition between professionals and amateurs. Whereas professional and amateur golfers have been competing in open tournaments for years, tennis federations steadfastly adhered to the principle that amateurs do not participate in tournaments with or against professionals. However, in 1968 England initiated the move to open play with the British Hardcourt Championships, followed by the first Wimbledon Open Championship. The reaction from both amateurs and professionals was enthusiastic, and other countries followed England's lead.

It is surprising how stable the rules, equipment, and scoring have remained from the development of the modern game to the present time. There have been occasional attempts to change parts of the game, particularly the system of scoring, but it is only recently that a change in scoring has been widely accepted.

It is relevant that the few outstanding tournament players in the United States today developed from the ranks of the hundreds of young players participating on public courts, in private clubs, in schools, and in community recreation programs. The game is no longer just for kings or the wealthy. Its popularity is increasing as people become more recreation-conscious and begin to recognize the value of the game.

HAVING TAKEN THE TIME TO READ THIS CHAPTER, YOU SHOULD HAVE LEARNED THAT:

Tennis has a long and colorful history, with the forerunner of the modern game evolving predominantly in France and England during the fifteenth and sixteenth centuries.

Tennis, in its modern form, was brought to the United States by Mary Outerbridge in 1874; by 1881, the USLTA had been formed and still remains the governing body of the game in the United States.

International team competition is represented by the Davis Cup, Wightman Cup, and Federation Cup Matches.

The four most prestigious tournaments in the world today are the Australian, French, Wimbledon (England), and United States Championships. Winning all of these tournaments in one season constitutes the "grand slam" of tennis.

6

BENEFITS
THAT MAY BE DERIVED
FROM TENNIS

After reading and studying this chapter, you should be more aware of the evidence concerning:
1. Possible physiological benefits of playing tennis
2. Possible psychological and social benefits of playing tennis

PHYSIOLOGICAL BENEFITS

No knowledgeable person doubts the contributions of physical activity to physical health. Regular physical activity results in more efficient pulmonary and cardio-vascular functioning, increased efficiency in the utilization of oxygen, and a lower incidence of coronary heart disease (Bradfield, 1968; Cooper, 1968). Evidence also points to the preventive aspects of regular exercise in the development of degenerative diseases such as coronary heart disease and atherosclerosis (Hein, 1960).

Evidence (Kozar and Hunsicker, 1963; Skubic and Hodgkins, 1967) indicates that reasonably vigorous tennis singles places a very real demand on the heart and circulatory system. Heart rates of 150-170 are typically recorded. The findings, in turn, mean that, at this rate, participation in singles at least three times a week should lead to significant gains in circulo-respiratory fitness (Sharkey and Holleman, 1967).

The increasing problem in the United States with obesity is a testament to the affluence and mechanization of our times. However, obesity has been demonstrated to provoke the onset of and to increase the severity of a number of chronic diseases (Bradfield, 1968). The significance of this point for the young adult and for the potential tennis player is that inactivity is being found to be a more important factor in obesity than previously believed.

Thus the physiological values to be derived from regular participation in tennis should be of more than passing interest. Though there are obviously some strength and muscular endurance gains for the arm, shoulder, and legs associated with regular participation in tennis, you would certainly not use tennis alone as a training program to increase strength and muscular endurance. Tennis improves endurance of the muscle groups involved *for the activity* involved much more than it improves the strength of those muscle groups. On the other hand, regular participation, especially in singles, can provide more than adequate exercise to significantly improve circulo-respiratory fitness. Since this is the kind of fitness most closely associated with prevention of coronary heart disease and with weight control, this is most important.

The average caloric cost of one hour of tennis singles is 2.6 calories per pound of body weight, some six to seven times greater than resting caloric cost. A 170-pound man, by playing just three times a week for an hour each day, could lose five pounds in ten weeks.

No one who has watched a grueling five-set match in the heat of the day could question the physiological demands of tennis. Watching or participating in such matches renews one's appreciation for the strength, endurance, and agility required. On the other hand, a player can, to some extent, control these demands. For example, a player can step onto the court for 30 minutes of rather casual hitting, an hour or two of moderately vigorous tennis, or perhaps only 15 minutes of a vigorous work-out, if time is limited. Being able to pattern the game to one's physical capacity is an advantage of tennis and a reason why players of all ages can participate. Thus, when played regularly, tennis can contribute substantially to physical fitness in terms of increased strength, increased endurance, and, particularly, cardio-vascular endurance. However, the physiological values derived depend on an individual's interest, level of skill, and intent.

PSYCHOLOGICAL AND SOCIAL BENEFITS

It is difficult to isolate and confirm what specific psychological and social gains can be derived from regular participation in any strenuous physical activity. Tennis is no exception; we feel intuitively that certain benefits are quite obvious for a given individual but, on the other hand, see the exact opposite effect in his opponent. The psychological and social benefits of activity, though they certainly do exist, are much more elusive, variable, and individualistic than are the physiological benefits just discussed.

Difficulty in generalizing about these psychological and social benefits does not make them less real. It simply means that we must couch the claims in slightly different terms. We must think in terms of what tennis *can* do and keep in mind that any of these benefits are highly variable, both qualitatively and quantitatively, and extremely dependent upon the individual. They may or may not be true for any given person. We can say, then, that regular participation in tennis *can* (Cowell, 1960; Scott, 1960);

1. provide a basis for changes in attitude toward oneself or toward life in general.

2. improve one's sense of well being.

3. contribute to positive mental health.

4. promote relaxation.

5. provide an outlet for tensions and anxieties.

6. provide relief for potential or existing psychosomatic disorders.

7. provide for growth in social relationships.

8. provide new friendships.

9. improve one's social status.

10. contribute to personal and social adjustment.

11. provide for simple enjoyment, if skill level is reasonably adequate.

12. provide opportunity to improve sportsmanship.

Menninger (1948) has said that "good mental health is directly related to the capacity and willingness of an individual to play." He further states that mentally healthy people generally "participate in some form of volitional activity" and that their "satisfaction from these activities meets deep seated psychological demands, quite beyond the superficial rationalization of enjoyment."

THIS CHAPTER CAN BE BRIEFLY SUMMARIZED BY SAYING THAT:

Tennis can increase muscular endurance and improve circulo-respiratory fitness, which may in turn reduce one's chances of developing coronary heart disease.

Tennis can contribute modestly to weight control or weight reduction programs (assuming caloric intake remains constant).

Tennis can contribute to one's psychological and social development in any of several ways, but its relative value in this regard varies with the individual.

7

THE MECHANICAL BASIS
OF TENNIS

This chapter will introduce you to:
1. The principle of angle of rebound
2. Linear and rotatory motion
and their relevance to tennis
3. The significance of range of motion
and the use of leverage in the stroke
4. The importance of the principles
of conservation of angular momentum and summation
of forces in developing good stroking patterns

Basic mechanical principles govern movement, whether it be movement of the human body, of an arrow in flight, or of an automobile speeding down the highway. The advocates of a principles approach to learning maintain that the individual who understands a theory or basic principle will be able to use this knowledge in solving many problems, while the individual who understands a few isolated facts is limited in the extent to which he can apply those facts. Unfortunately, studies do not consistently support this approach (Cratty, 1964). Yet, so much of the positioning and movement used in tennis is based on rather simple mechanical principles that it is felt an awareness of some of these principles will facilitate the learning process.

ANGLES OF REBOUND AND SPIN

An object rebounds from a surface at the same angle at which it strikes that surface. This principle has direct relevance to the tennis situation in regard to the rebound of the ball from the court surface and also from the racket. In regard to the rebound from the court, the principle must be qualified slightly in order to be completely accurate. Because of the softness of a tennis ball, the angle of rebound from the court surface is slightly less than the angle at which it contacted the surface.

There are three phases to a ball's rebound from the court. During the first phase the ball is rising, during the second phase it is at the top of the ascent, and during the third phase it is descending. The most advantageous point at which to hit the ball is at the top of its rise, before it begins descending. Players must thus learn to position themselves to contact the ball at this point whenever possible, a task that implies an awareness of rebound and for which proper footwork is essential.

The angle of the racket face at the moment of contact with the ball determines the trajectory of the ball. Most balls should be contacted with the racket held perpendicular to the court. If a ball is contacted on the descent and below hip level, the angle of the racket face may have to be adjusted to a slightly open position. This is particularly true when hitting a volley which has dropped below the level of the net. However, if the ball is hit at waist height with the racket face open, the flight of the ball is much higher than is normally desirable. *This action is one of the most frequent hitting errors of beginning players!* If it is necessary to contact the ball above shoulder level, the racket face should be slightly closed or angled downward. If the ball is met at waist height and the racket face is closed, balls tend to go into the net. The beginning player should attempt to contact most balls at waist height with the racket face perpendicular to the court surface or in a slightly open position. (This position may vary somewhat with the height of the players.)

LINEAR AND ROTATORY MOTION

If a ball is contacted at its center and the racket moves in a straight line while it is in contact with the ball, the flight of the ball is a straight line—that is, linear motion results. The ball will continue to travel in a straight line until air resistance and gravity force it downward. If the ball is contacted off center, rotatory motion results, that is, the ball spins.

In tennis, rotatory motion is frequently desired and the ball is hit off-center or the racket is drawn across the ball at the moment of impact to impart topspin, backspin, or lateral spin. Each type of spin affects the bounce of the ball in a different manner. If a ball is hit with topspin, it rotates

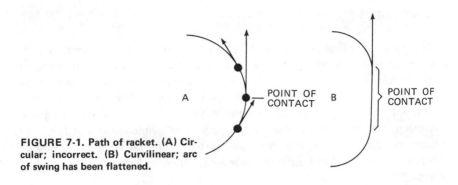

FIGURE 7-1. Path of racket. (A) Circular; incorrect. (B) Curvilinear; arc of swing has been flattened.

forward in relation to its line of direction. The spin pulls the ball down to the court abruptly and the rebound is higher than a rebound without spin. If a ball is hit with backspin, it rotates backward—or away from its line of direction. It tends to rise slightly before bouncing, and the bounce is closer to the vertical plane than the bounce of a ball with no spin. A ball hit with lateral spin rotates sideways. It curves the direction it is rotating.

Although the player should have some awareness of the effects of spin, *the beginning player should not be concerned with trying to impart spin*. He should concentrate on developing a stroke in which the ball is met at the center and the arm and racket move in a linear path through the hitting range. After developing a solid hit with maximum control, attention can be given to methods of imparting spin.

The movement of the racket and arm in the forehand and backhand drives is a combination of rotatory and curvilinear motion. This means that the motion of the arm and racket during a forehand drive, for example, does not follow a strictly circular path, but a path in which the arc of the swing is flattened. Fig. 7-1A shows a circular path as though viewing a tennis swing from above. With this movement pattern there is only one point at which the racket could contact the ball and yield successful results. In reality, the arc of the swing is flattened, as shown in Fig. 7-1B. This arc has a greater range in which the ball can be contacted for a controlled hit. It also enables the racket to move in a straight line through the hitting range, which aids in hitting the ball straight. This arc also enables the racket to remain in contact with the ball longer, an essential factor in good stroke development. A step forward on the foot opposite the hitting arm also flattens the arc of the swing, adds to the linear motion, and helps keep the ball in contact with the strings slightly longer.

RANGE OF MOTION

Increasing the range of motion of a stroke increases the momentum with which an object is contacted, and thus the force imparted to an object is greater. However, in tennis control is a predominant factor in learning the skills and it is felt that the force with which the ball is hit is secondary to the need for control—at least through the beginning and intermediate stages of learning. For this reason, the learning sequences employed in this book are based on the principle that, through shortening the backswing, the coordination involved in hitting the ball is lessened, thereby lessening the chance of error.

LEVERAGE

The mechanical action of hitting a tennis ball is basically one of applied leverage. The arm is a series of levers and the addition of a racket increases the over-all length of these levers. As you probably know, increasing the length of the lever increases the force which can be generated at the end of the lever. Analyzing the leverage action employed in tennis only this far, however, may leave the erroneous impression that most of the movement consists of hitting with a completely extended arm and a straight line from the shoulder through the racket. However, in most of the strokes there should be a slight flexion of the elbow on the backswing and forward swing. With the serve there is maximum flexion at the elbow immediately prior to contacting the ball, followed by flexion at the wrist as contact is made. Such positions create a shorter lever but utilize the principle of *conservation of angular momentum*. This principle simply means that since the lever is shorter it can be moved through the radius of the swing with greater speed. Since the force with which the ball is hit is related to the speed of the swing, hitting with a shorter lever traveling through a smaller arc and therefore with more speed should impart a force at least equal to, if not greater, than that developed with a long lever (Cooper, 1968).

Also, the principle of *summation of forces* should be considered in relation to the leverage action of tennis strokes. Summation of forces refers to the use of several joints successively rather than simultaneously. When speed is required at an extremity, the joints work in sequence, with the force of each subsequent joint being added to the force of the preceding one. This principle is used in the serve. More force can be generated in the serve by using the shoulder, upper arm, lower arm, and wrist sequentially than it is possible to generate with all parts moving together. This principle can also be applied to the forehand and backhand drives, although the application is more relevant for the advanced player who uses some wrist snap at the point of contact with the ball. Since control is harder to maintain with wrist snap, *it is recommended that beginning and intermediate players keep a firm wrist throughout the stroke.*

AFTER COMPLETING THIS CHAPTER, YOU SHOULD UNDERSTAND:

How to hit the ball with little or no ball spin and what effect spin has on the flight and rebound of the ball.

What effect a closed or open racket face has on the flight of the ball.

Why the forehand and backhand strokes should follow a curvilinear rather than a curved path.

Why the ball is not contacted with the arm and racket completely extended to the side on the forehand and backhand drives.

Why the arm and shoulder are used sequentially in stroking rather than as one unit.

8

THE DEVELOPMENT OF MOTOR SKILL

After studying this chapter, you should:
1. Be familiar with some of the basic
   concepts of motor learning
2. Be able to adapt these concepts
   to the learning of tennis

The acquisition of any skill which involves body movement is referred to as motor learning. It is felt that you will be able to approach the task of learning tennis more realistically with an awareness of some of the problems basic to the development of motor skills. Therefore, we first consider some perceptual-motor aspects of skill development particularly relevant to the learning of tennis. Secondly, factors which affect the learning situation are discussed.

PERCEPTUAL-MOTOR ASPECTS OF SKILL DEVELOPMENT

The multitude of movements you will make in learning to play tennis will be the result of perception. Perception is a process whereby a variety of sensory data, derived from sources such as the eyes, the ears, and the tactile receptors of the skin, are organized in the brain to provide meaning to the sensations and serve as a basis for determining the appropriate motor response. In terms of learning tennis skills, a visual perception might be that of an approaching tennis ball. The continued perceptual organization provides information as to the direction from which the

ball is approaching and the speed of its flight. In response to these percep-
tions, preparations are made to return the ball. The faulty judgments we
sometimes make in attempting to hit a tennis ball are often the result of
inaccurate visual perception.

Perceptual abilities are enhanced by the use of *cues*. Visual cues, for
example, help us determine how fast the ball is coming, how far we must
move to hit it, or even how high the bounce may be. Players learn that if a
ball is hit high, it will have a high bounce, and they should immediately begin
moving into proper position for the return. The height of the ball thus serves
as a "cue" for them to begin making the necessary spatial adjustments. If the
player waited for the ball to bounce to see how high it would rebound, it
would be too late to get into position to return it. As players become experienced, they learn that they must begin moving into position as soon as the
ball leaves the racket of the opposing player and they can determine its
direction. Interpreting visual cues quickly gives a player more time to get into
position and is part of what players term *anticipation*.

Thus far we have talked only about external cues. Internal cues, however,
may be even more helpful in the learning of motor skills than external cues.
For example, the brain is constantly made aware of body position and movement through sensations such as weight, tensions, pressure, and speed of
movement. This sense of movement and position is called the *kinesthetic
sense*. Without this sense, it would be impossible to undertake as simple a
movement as walking without carefully watching every movement of each
foot, thereby replacing kinesthetic cues with visual cues.

In illustration of this sense, we find reference is often made to getting the
"feel" of certain positions. For example, one must develop a feel for the
proper forehand and backhand grips. Since it would be wholly impractical to
have to look at the hand on the racket each time a grip change was made for
visual feedback, the player perceives sensations of the racket against the palm
and fingers and learns to recognize immediately if it is an incorrect position.
In developing a forehand drive it is suggested that a beginning player perform
a drill to learn the proper position for the racket and body at the precise
moment contact is made with the ball. Visual cues can be used initially, such
as looking to see if the racket head is even with or slightly above the wrist,
but the use of kinesthetic cues is more important. How does the position
feel? What sensations are created in the wrist and in the forearm when the
ball contacts the racket? As with the grip, an awareness of the feeling of the
right position and movement can be developed through kinesthetic feedback,
and eventually you will be able to tell whether your stroke was good or bad
by the way it felt.

FACTORS AFFECTING THE LEARNING SITUATION

Motivation

People learn to play tennis for a variety of reasons. Some want to play to develop or maintain fitness, others want to learn because their girl friend or boy friend plays, and still others desire the competitive challenge tennis provides. One of the most widely accepted principles of learning is that an individual must be interested in a particular task before effective learning can occur. Therefore, it is reasonable to assume that if you *want* to play tennis, your chances of learning to play are much improved. If you are taking a tennis class merely to fulfill a university requirement or because someone else wants you to learn, although you have no particular interest in the game, your chances of developing the necessary skills are considerably diminished.

Preparatory Set

One of the first steps the learner can take when attempting to learn a new skill is to develop a *set* (a readiness to act, an expectancy, or a preparation to learn). A teacher may develop a preparatory set among students by giving preperformance verbal instructions, by a demonstration, or by having students assume a particular position as preparation for the movement to follow (Hilgard, 1967). The learner, however, does not have to depend on the teacher for the development of set. For example, when working on a forehand drive in tennis, the performer can increase his readiness by conceptualizing or thinking through the movement he is about to perform. In addition, he can physically and mentally assume a state of readiness.

Reinforcement

Reinforcement is an event or a condition which strengthens the probability of a response. In the laboratory an animal presses a lever and receives a pellet of food. The pellet is a reinforcer and increases the probability that the animal will press the lever again. The value of reinforcement in learning motor skills is primarily motivational. It implies that the learner should have the kind of success experiences which encourage him to continue. This means that the task should be sequentially structured so that success can be achieved at one step which will motivate the learner to progress to the next.

Feedback

Experimental evidence clearly indicates that knowledge of correct performance, gained through feedback, rapidly improves the learning of a performance pattern (McDonald, 1965). This feedback can be *internal* or *external*, *concurrent* or *delayed*. When playing tennis, a player hits the ball and can immediately see if the ball goes where he intended it to go. This feedback is visual, and therefore internal, and concurrent, since the knowledge of results is immediate. In contrast, an instructor sometimes watches a performer and provides analytical comments about his performance. For example, a tennis instructor might direct a player to start the backswing sooner or to keep the racket head higher through a stroke. This example is also concurrent, but it is external, rather than internal, since it comes from a source other than the performer.

Concurrent feedback has been shown to be of more value to the learner than delayed feedback (feedback given the performer sometime after the performance). One researcher (Robb, 1966) found that concurrent visual feedback was the most important variable in learning a specified movement pattern. Similarly, internal feedback is more important to a learner than external feedback. Highly skilled players have learned to make more effective use of internal feedback than have beginners. The former respond more accurately to the internal cues which tell them that their racket has reached the point of maximum backswing on a forehand drive or that their elbow is not bending sufficiently during the service motion or that they are not bending their knees enough to get into position for strokes.

Mental Practice

A phenomenon of which educators have had some awareness for several years but which has not yet been systematically incorporated into teaching situations to a large degree is that referred to as *mental practice*. As early as the 1930s, electrophysiological studies showed that when subjects imagined they were performing a particular motor response, the muscles which would be used in the overt performance of that motor task were subconsciously flexing. The concept of mental practice, developed from this basis, consists of mentally rehearsing a motor skill through imagining the movement to be performed (visual imagery) or through a verbal description or conceptualization of the movement.

Considerable evidence shows that mental practice can aid in the learning of a movement pattern (Oxendine, 1968). The research, however, has been consistent in indicating that physical practice is of primary importance and that mental practice should be supplemental to it rather than a substitute for it. In addition, it is consistent in indicating that, for mental practice to be effective, there must be knowledge of the skill to be performed (Oxendine, 1968).

Practice Schedules

Practice schedules generally involve either *massed practice*—intensive practice without rest between trials—or *distributed practice*—trials interspersed with rest periods. Considerable research indicates that distributed practice is of greater value (Hilgard, 1967; McDonald, 1965).

Two factors which must be considered in any practice session are fatigue and loss of motivation. For example, if a player is practicing a volley in tennis, after a period of time the muscles of the forearm would tire sufficiently to hinder performance. Also, although intensive practice may cause an initial increase in motivation, motivation generally decreases as the practice session becomes longer. It is essentially a matter of the performer becoming bored with a particular activity after a period of time.

It is also known that the longer the time between practice sessions, the greater the loss in performance skill (McDonald, 1965). Therefore, several practice sessions during a week yield greater results in terms of desired performance than practicing once a week, even if the time spent in one practice is equivalent to the several shorter sessions. However, as an individual's level of skill improves, it is possible for him to derive beneficial results from longer practice sessions; the very highly skilled tennis player frequently spends several hours in practice. It can be assumed that his motivation for improvement is greater than that of most beginners and that he is in better physical condition for sustained performance. Therefore, factors such as strength and endurance levels, skill, and strength of motivation have to be considered in the establishment of practice schedules.

YOU SHOULD NOW KNOW THAT:

Perception is a basic factor in the development of motor skills.

An individual with a strong desire to play tennis has a greater chance of learning than an individual who is not similarly motivated.

The learner can facilitate the learning situation by developing a set, or a readiness to act, and by verbally conceptualizing or mentally rehearsing a skill.

Concurrent and internal feedback are more effective in altering future performance than are external and delayed feedback.

Distributed practice is generally more beneficial to a beginning tennis player than massed practice.

9

CONDITIONING FOR TENNIS

After reading this chapter, you should know:
1. *That the will to win is an important factor in any athletic contest, but not as important as the will to prepare to win*
2. *The importance of physical conditioning to skilled play*
3. *Several conditioning drills for developing ground strokes, the serve, the volley, and the overhead*

GENERAL PHYSICAL CONDITIONING

The same principles of general physical conditioning apply to competitive tennis players as to competitors in other sports activities. Strength, muscular endurance, cardio-vascular endurance, flexibility, and agility are necessary for advanced play. Activities which develop cardio-vascular endurance, such as distance running, speed sprints, and rope jumping, are excellent conditioners for tennis. Short sprints with numerous changes of direction are also beneficial since they simulate movement in the game situation. For example, players may run from one side of a court to another as quickly as they can and maintain the activity for a reasonable length of time. Weight training is beneficial in developing strength and should be directed toward the muscles of the arms, shoulders, chest, and, to a lesser extent, the legs. It is felt that isometric activities have limited value. If one understood the principles of isometric activity, certain exercises could be used advantageously, but only as a supplement to a general conditioning program based essentially on the development of cardio-vascular endurance.

So much information is available to the interested reader concerning general physical conditioning that it seems unnecessary to give it detailed treatment here. We have selected instead to discuss advanced drills, performed on a tennis court, which develop physical fitness and, at the same time, provide practice on the strokes and on ball placement.

Ground Strokes

1. One of the better drills for ground strokes is to place two players at opposite ends of the court. Instruct Player A to hit all balls cross court and Player B to hit all balls down the line. Each must try to hit the balls solidly and consistently keep them in the court.

This drill requires that each player run the full width of the court, properly position himself to hit the ball to the designated position, then quickly sprint to the opposite side of the court for the return. After 15 or 20 minutes the players can alternate shots so that Player A hits down the line and Player B hits cross court. The obvious advantage of this drill is that both players hit more forehand and backhand placement shots in a few minutes than they normally would during hours of play.

The second advantage is found in the physical requirements of the drill. All shots are hit after short sprints and quick stops in the proper position from which to execute the shot correctly. The player must then sprint to the opposite side and repeat the cycle. This drill is excellent for improving drives, placements, and footwork. It also develops leg strength, speed, and endurance.

2. Another drill to improve backcourt proficiency is to have both players play actual points from the back court and allow them to advance to the net only on short or weak returns. This drill conditions physically, as the points are considerably longer than the serving and volley type game. It also conditions mentally, as it requires concentration for considerably longer periods of time than usual game points. In addition, it assists players in developing court strategy and offers them the opportunity to practice better approach shots.

Serving and Returning Drills

1. Serving a basket or two of balls before play each day is an excellent drill for beginners and intermediate players. It strengthens the arm, back, and

shoulder muscles and assists in the development of a smooth, accurate service motion.

2. A variation of this service drill is often used by more advanced players. Place two servers on one side of the court with a basket of balls and one receiver on the opposite side to return serves. The servers alternate serving and advancing to the net behind the serve to practice their first volley. The receiver simply attempts to get a consistent return of serve and occasionally follows his return to the net.

This drill affords each player the opportunity of hitting more serves and service returns in a short period of time than he might normally experience during a match. The continued serving strengthens the arm and improves consistency and accuracy. Sprinting to the net behind the serve and quickly stopping to volley strengthens the legs and knees. It also helps the server move to the net and assume volleying position faster.

Volley and Overhead Drills

Beginning and intermediate players can place themselves at the net to continually practice the mechanics of the volley and overhead shots. The continuous repetition develops control. The advanced player, however, must rely on more than simply being consistent at the net. He must move fast and have quick reflexes and sufficient stamina to maintain net play over a period of time. A player that tends to tire in the least degree eventually fails to get into proper position and consequently errs.

1. Two players stand on opposite sides of and six feet back from the net. They volley back and forth, keeping the ball in play and gradually increasing the force of the hits. This drill develops reaction time and speed of movement.

2. Place a net player six feet from the net opposite a ball hitter with a large basket of balls. The hitter should begin at about the service line and gradually move forward. The hitter should drive balls from side to side allowing the net player just enough time to reach the ball and position himself for the next return. Occasionally a lob should be used to keep the net player alert and to force him to move into proper position for the overhead. The speed and number of balls hit must be adapted to the ability of the player but must consistently challenge him to capacity. Gradually increasing the speed, number of balls, angle of the hit, and closeness of the hitter to the net man forces the net player to move quicker and develop faster reflexes.

IN SUMMARY:

Tennis skills improve faster if associated with conditioning drills and exercises to develop strength, endurance, agility, and reaction time.

Drills can be devised to develop physical conditioning while simultaneously providing practice on selected strokes, placement, and footwork.

Physical conditioning plays an important part in the success of tournament players.

10

ADVANCED STROKES
AND STRATEGY

Now that you have learned the basic game of tennis,
this chapter covers:
1. The mechanics and the advantages of the
half volley, the lob, the overhead smash,
the drop shot, and putting spin on serves
2. Some basic strategy for the novice
3. Positioning and patterns of play
in both singles and doubles

ADVANCED STROKES

The Half Volley

The half volley is a short stroke or half stroke used to hit a ball immediately after it bounces. This stroke is generally used by a player as he approaches the net and is unable to get into proper position to volley the ball. Therefore, the half volley is a defensive stroke.

The proper execution of the half volley requires the wrist to break to the contact point and remain firm in that position, the knees to bend sufficiently so that the head of the racket is approximately even with the ball, and contact to be made with the ball immediately after it bounces and starts its rise. It must be emphasized that the player must bend his knees to get down to the ball instead of standing straight and allowing the racket head to drop.

The racket moves forward following impact in a short follow through. If the player is close to the service line, the follow through is a short movement in the direction of the hit. If he is near the base line, the ball needs added momentum to travel the additional distance, and the follow through is proportionately longer.

Since the half volley is a defensive stroke, it should be avoided whenever the player can get into position to volley the ball or to hit a proper ground stroke. It should be used only when the player is trapped and has no other alternative.

A half volley can be practiced by standing near the service line and having a partner hit balls at your feet. The practice should be focused on controlling the direction of the hit; since there is no backswing, there is little power to a half volley.

The Lob

A lob is hit high into the air and drops deep into the opponent's court near the baseline. Its purpose is to move an opponent away from the net or to pass an opponent by placing the ball over his head and out of reach.

Lobs are hit similar to forehand and backhand drives. Whereas the stroking pattern is basically the same, the racket face is in a more open position to direct the ball to the desired height. Since the stroke is based on finesse rather than on power, a long backswing is unnecessary. Since the follow through should be a natural continuation of the stroke, the follow through is higher than for a drive.

A lob can be used offensively or defensively. A defensive lob is generally used by a player who has been pulled out of the court and is unable to get into proper position to hit a drive. The object is to hit the ball high into the air, which moves the opposing player away from the net and allows ample time for the lobbing player to return to the court and assume a proper court position.

An offensive lob is used to hit the ball over the opponent's head for a placement or for a passing shot. The object is to hit the ball so that it barely clears the height to which the opposing player can reach and drops near the base line. If the ball goes too high, it gives the opposing player an opportunity to get into position for a return. If it fails to go high enough, it will most likely be returned with an overhead smash. For this reason, it is advisable to lob to the opponent's backhand side, since an overhead taken from the backhand side is less effective than one taken from the forehand side. Deception must be used when executing this shot as it is essential that an opponent be caught off guard and not have time to move into position for the overhead smash. Therefore, most offensive lobs are hit from a position inside the court where the player has the option of various alternatives and can employ an element of surprise.

Players should practice hitting lobs from various court positions with both forehand and backhand strokes. Experiment with the angle of the racket face to learn to control the height of the ball.

The Overhead Smash

The overhead smash is the answer to a lob, since it is a hard downward hit of a high ball. When properly executed the smash generally wins the point, since both power and placement can be achieved.

The motion, the mechanical principles, and the grip exhibited in the overhead smash are the same as those used for the serve, that is, the eastern grip for many beginning players and the continental grip for most intermediate and advanced players. The position for the overhead smash is sideways to the net, with the racket head above the head and pointing in the direction of the descending ball. To facilitate the fast movement necessary to get into position, the player must turn sideways as the lob is hit and quickly sidestep into position. As the ball starts its downward movement, the racket head drops back and the elbow bends, which guides the racket into the back scratching position described for the serve. When the ball approaches hitting range, the racket is brought into contact position by a vigorous extension of the elbow. The arm straightens, and the wrist snaps forward to contact the ball. As contact is made, the wrist continues to move forward and downward while the weight transfers from the rear to the forward foot. The shoulders and hips rotate forward and to the left in the same follow through that accompanies the serve.

The success of this shot depends on proper timing. The player must know the precise moment to initiate the backswing to keep the racket and arm in continuous motion throughout the stroke. The stroke must also be timed so that the ball is contacted with the arm fully extended and at a point slightly forward of the shoulders. If the ball is contacted too far forward, the hit will go into the net; if the ball is contacted behind the line of the shoulder, the trajectory of the ball will be high or parallel with the court rather than downward.

Since the overhead smash is a difficult stroke requiring precise timing, it must be practiced regularly to assure proficiency.

The Drop Shot

The drop shot travels close to the top of the net, then drops sharply to the court, and has a low, almost vertical bounce. The efficacy of this shot lies not only in the finesse or skill with which it can be executed but also in the element of surprise which generally accompanies its use.

The beginning movements of a drop shot are similar to those of a forehand or backhand drive. At the instant before contact the racket face opens slightly and the racket, while continuing to move forward, is drawn down the back of the ball to impart backspin, the key to the desired action. The backspin causes the ball to move through the air at a slightly slower speed; the rotating action causes the ball to drop faster than would be expected if it had no spin; and the backspin results in a low ball bounce in a near vertical plane.

The effectiveness of the drop shot lies in imparting just the correct amount of backspin to achieve a hit which looks as though it is going to be a drive but which drops sharply as it crosses the net.

Drop shots are more effective on a slow surface, such as clay, or on grass courts, which have a characteristically low bounce, than they are on hardcourts.

The Serve

One of the most common errors made by the beginning and intermediate player is attempting to hit the first serve as hard and flat as he possibly can, while "tapping" the second serve to assure its going into the proper service court. Few tournament players deliver many serves as hard as they can or completely devoid of spin. Serving at maximum speed is tiring during the course of a match and the flat serve is harder to control than a serve with spin. Consequently, the advanced player varies his serves. The three deliveries generally used are (1) the flat serve, (2) the slice serve, and (3) the twist serve. The one a player chooses at a specified time depends upon the power he desires and the margin of safety and control he feels is necessary. All three serves are hit with the service grip described in Chapter 4.

The flat serve. To hit a flat serve, the racket must strike the ball from directly behind and at about the center of the ball as shown in Fig. 10-1, to give forward and downward momentum with little or no spin. The advantage of this serve is that it can be hit with tremendous speed; some serves have been clocked at well over 100 miles per hour. The disadvantage is that a hard hit ball must travel close to the top of the net in order to drop into the service court. Consequently, there is little margin for error and many faults are made.

The slice serve. Most tournament players impart a slight amount of slice to

FIGURE 10-1. Contact point for flat serve

their serves. This slice is partially due to the use of the continental grip, which puts the racket face at an angle whereby slight spin naturally occurs, and partially due to the ball throw. The racket face is at an angle as it meets the ball, as shown in Fig. 10-2. In addition, the racket face strikes slightly to the right side (from the server's position) of the ball rather than at the center of the ball. This off-center hit imparts a sideward, or lateral, spin which causes the ball to drop faster and to carry to the receiver's right side. Because of the spin, a player has a greater margin of safety and can hit it higher across the net. Since a spinning ball tends to drop faster than a ball hit with no spin, the chances are greater that it will remain within the boundaries of the proper service court.

Occasionally the server may impart a great amount of side spin to the ball by throwing it farther to his right and emphasizing the hit or brush along the right side of the ball. This serve tends to bounce away from the receiver, drawing him into the alley when he is receiving in his right service court. However, the additional spin further slows the speed of the ball and the player must decide whether the additional spin is worth the diminished speed. A heavily sliced ball is not recommended for consistent use, but it can be an effective change of pace.

FIGURE 10-2. Contact point for slice serve

The American twist. The American twist is a serve which imparts top spin with a slight amount of lateral spin. It is difficult to learn and extremely tiring if used consistently, yet it can be highly effective. To impart the desired spin, the ball is tossed slightly behind the *left* side of the body. If the ball were thrown into the proper position but not contacted, it would drop behind the left shoulder of the server if he were assuming a proper serving stance. Hitting the ball in this position necessitates arching the back as shown in Fig. 10-3. With the back arched and the racket moving from the back-scratching position, the racket brushes up the back of the ball and imparts

FIGURE 10-3. Contact point for American twist serve

top spin. However, in addition to brushing upward, the arm and racket are also moving from left to right, which imparts some lateral spin.

The ball passes high across the net and allows a large margin of safety. Topspin or forward spin on a ball causes it to descend more abruptly than a ball with no spin and brings it into the service court. The spin also affects the rebound; the ball has a faster and higher bounce than would be expected from a serve with no spin. Players refer to this action as a "kick"—the ball kicks high and to the receiver's left side, which again pulls him out of position.

The advantage of the twist serve is that it is in the air a longer time than other serves, which allows a net rusher more time to get into proper position at the net. When executed properly, it is a consistent serve. However, it is a difficult serve to learn and often falls shallow in the service court, which allows an easier return.

Objectives of the serve. The server's major objective is to get the first serve into the court with both power and placement and with 70 to 80 percent accuracy. The second serve should be hit about *as hard as the first serve* but with more spin to allow a greater margin of safety. The second serve should have near 100 percent reliability to avoid giving points away through needless double faults.

The speed of the serve and the amount of spin imparted should be varied. The server must decide in advance how hard to serve the ball, how much spin to impart, and to what position he will serve. He must watch the ball at all times and not be annoyed by any last minute movements or adjustments of the receiver.

COURT POSITION AND BASIC STRATEGY

Basic Strategy for the Novice

For the novice, a basic rule of strategy is to keep the ball in play. Learn to return the ball to your opponent's court consistently from any position with both forehand and backhand shots. Do not worry about speed or placement initially; return the ball—keep it in play. Hard drives, accurate placements, and sharp angles can be developed as your skill progresses. It must be remembered that the most highly skilled players first developed the ability to return every type of shot consistently.

The novice often has the idea that every hit should be a drive of sufficient force to barely skim the top of the net and carry to the base line. The world's top competitors can manage this type of drive repeatedly, but for the less skilled it is suggested that more clearance be allowed. If a ball is hit barely to clear the net, there is little margin for error and the hit must be accurate within a few inches. Since few novices are that accurate, it is wise to allow four to five feet clearance on drives. This clearance increases the margin for error and results in fewer balls being hit into the net. Likewise, if a player aims within one or two inches of the side lines, he is allowing little margin for error. He can safely allow five to six feet leeway and still move an opponent back and forth across the court.

Position for Singles Play

The server should serve from behind the base line next to the center mark. His objective is to win the point outright, force an error, or keep the receiver off balance and thereby force a weak return. The receiver should stand near the base line about two feet from the singles side line. He can move forward or backward depending on the speed and type of serve he must return. His objective is to return the ball back to the side of the court or low at the server's feet if the server is following his serve to the net or deep into the court if the server elects to stay in the back court. Any of these returns take the advantage away from the server and place him on the defensive.

The proper location for singles play during the point is behind the base line in the center of the court or six to eight feet from the net in a volleying position. From the base line position, the player can move freely to either side to return balls close to the side lines; he can move back two or three steps to get into position to hit the difficult deep shot; or he can move forward to intercept a short ball or a drop shot. After each shot, the player should return to his original position behind the base line or at the net to properly prepare to return the next ball. A player who consistently returns to the proper location returns more balls, makes fewer errors, and wins more points.

Another mistake often made by the beginner is to try to play from a position in the center of the court. This position, halfway between the base line and the net, is acceptable for a beginner trying to develop his stroke but should never be used in a playing situation. The position does not allow the player adequate time to move back to return deep balls and forces him to hit many balls which are low and at his feet. These types of shots, low volleys and half volleys, require considerably more timing and coordination to execute properly and are generally defensive in nature. Consequently, this position on the court has become known as "no man's land," which is a way of saying that it is a poor position to be caught in.

Advance to the Net on Good Shots

For the intermediate and advanced players, most points are won by hitting outright winners or by forcing your opponent to err. A player who has successfully mastered the net game has a distinct advantage in both of these areas. If he hits a strong forcing serve, he can move to the net and attempt to volley the weak return. He can also take any short return, drive it deep into his opponent's court, and then move to the net. In either case, the offensive advantage is with the player at the net; his opponent must hit a "great shot" to win the point or take the chance of having a weak return "cut off" or volleyed by the net man. However, it must be remembered that a player attempting to advance to the net must choose his shots carefully. If he moves to the net when his opponent is neither forced nor rushed, he stands a good chance of being passed as his opponent carefully hits to the side lines or lobs a ball over his head.

Positioning for Doubles

In doubles play, the rules do not specify where the two partners must stand after the ball has been served. They can both be at the net, both stay back, or play one up and one back. The positions of play selected and the basic strategies chosen depend entirely on the ability and stage of development of the players. For example, advanced players, who can hit all types of shots, prefer to position themselves in such a manner as to facilitate movement to the net, where they have the greatest chance of winning the point. In such a position as that in Fig. 10-4 the server serves from behind the base line about five feet from the singles side line. The server's partner stands about six feet from the net and three feet in from the singles side line. The net man faces the player about to receive the serve. The objective of the server is to advance to the net after his serve, establish position at the net with his partner, and attempt to volley the ball for a placement or force an error.

The receiver stands slightly inside the base line about two feet from the singles side line. The receiver's partner stands at the net facing the server. The objective of the receiver is to return the serve low at the feet of the advancing server and move to the net to establish position with his partner, volley the ball for a placement or force an error. In advanced doubles play—with all players advancing to the net—the advantage is always with the serving team. Consequently, many matches are prolonged for hours before a player's service is broken or lost unless the "sudden death" tie-breaker rule is in effect.

In beginning tennis, the server's partner and the receiver's partner need not be at the net. The determining factors are the players' knowledge and ability

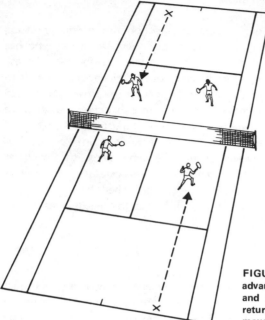

FIGURE 10-4. Basic positioning for advanced doubles play. Server serves and moves to net position; receiver returns ball to advancing server and moves to net position.

to play the net effectively. If a beginner does not feel comfortable at the net, he may move back with the receiver, or server, and play from the back court until he develops more confidence in his net game. Fig. 10-5 shows a pattern of play often preferred by the beginner. The partners of both the server and the receiver play at the net, while the server and receiver stay back to cover their half of the court. The objective of both teams is to keep the ball away from the net and in the back court in hopes of forcing an error. Both net men pose a potential threat, as they can at any time move across court to volley a weak return. The exact pattern of play changes with the ability of the players. An effort should be made to learn to play the net effectively as many advantages can be gained from this position.

USE YOUR HEAD IN TENNIS

One often hears the comment, "He is a beautiful player with sound strokes. I wonder why he never wins?" The answer to this question is generally found, not in the strokes themselves but in the patterns of play or shots which the

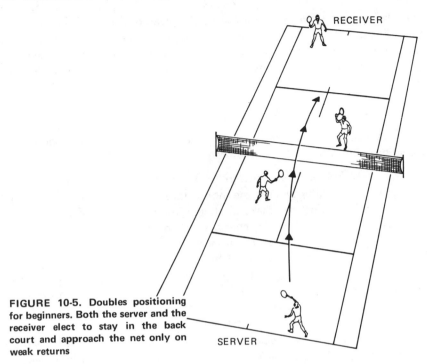

FIGURE 10-5. Doubles positioning for beginners. Both the server and the receiver elect to stay in the back court and approach the net only on weak returns

player elects to use. There is more to being a good player than simply being able to hit the ball with the proper strokes. A good player knows when to hit the ball hard, when to ease up, when to be cautious, and when to take chances.

Percentage Tennis

Percentage tennis is best described as the ability to hit the shot or pattern of shots that provides the greatest chance of winning the point. For example, assume you are playing a beginner who is trying to hit the ball hard toward the sidelines. You can win points by simply keeping the ball in play and allowing your opponent to attempt the hard shots to the corners. The shots he has selected are low percentage shots for his ability. He will eventually make far more errors than placements and consequently defeat himself.

Too often, beginning and intermediate players feel that every shot should be a point-winning shot. Obviously, every shot cannot result in the winning of a point. Instead, every hit should serve one of three functions. It should (1) keep the ball safely in play while you wait for an opportunity for the put-away shot or the point winner, (2) put a player in a better position strategically, or (3) serve as the put-away shot or the point winner. Playing percentage tennis is learning what shot to attempt in a given situation in relation to your level of skill.

Selecting a Pattern of Play

Before selecting a pattern of play or the shots to be used, consideration should be given to the following factors:

1. *Can I hit the shot consistently?* In selecting a particular shot, a player must analyze his ability to make the shot and weigh the advantages of making it against the errors he may make in attempting it. For example, a drop shot is particularly effective on a clay court against an opponent near the base line. It may constitute the ideal return; however, if a player has not been practicing that shot or is not confident of his ability to make it successfully, his chances for error are great. He must therefore weigh his ability to execute a drop shot against the errors he may make in attempting it. On this basis he can select to attempt the shot or can choose an alternative. A good player selects the shot that yields the highest percentage for success.

2. *If a shot is executed properly will it win the point or place me in a more favorable position?* Many players increase their chance for error by attempting a difficult shot when it is unnecessary. A player must take some chances when playing percentage tennis, but when a chance is taken, the player should either win the point or at least put himself in better position strategically. If a shot accomplishes neither, the chance has not been worth taking. For example, if a player is caught behind the base line with an opponent in good position at the net, it would be foolish for him to attempt a power drive down the sideline. The chances for error in such a shot are high, and the chances are also good that a net player would be able to cut off such a return anyway. Therefore, a different return would give better odds.

Many players also choose to hit difficult shots to win the point when it is unnecessary to do so. For example, a player may have hit a shot or pattern of shots that pulled his opponent off the court—entirely out of position. All that is required to win the point is a simple return almost anywhere within the opponent's court. But, instead of the simple, safe return, the player may attempt a more colorful power shot, or the suspenseful drop volley. Either may be successful, but the probability for error is far greater than with the simple return. Do not take chances when it is unnecessary to do so!

3. *What are the strengths and weaknesses of my opponent?* The way you

play your game—the patterns of shots you choose—may be influenced by the game played by your opponent. You should therefore know both his strengths and his weaknesses.

You often hear the adage, "Take advantage of your opponent's weaknesses." This statement should be qualified by "*. . . on the crucial points.*" Rather than constantly playing a weakness, wait for the crucial point or the crucial shot in an exchange to apply pressure to that weakness. If a player is known to have a weak backhand, the first few exchanges may alternate to his forehand and backhand, but as you maneuver your opponent out of position or move yourself into position to rush the net, hit the next shot deep to the backhand corner. Your opponent will not only have to return the ball from his weak side, but he will also be forced to move quickly to get into position and to hit cautiously enough to keep his return away from you. If you repeatedly play into a weak stroke, you run the risk of getting your opponent "grooved," or set, for that return, and consequently the weakness builds into a strength.

The physical condition of an opponent can be a significant factor in the outcome of a match. A player should know whether an opponent can last through five sets, or three sets for women competitors, without tiring. If your opponent is noted for tiring in a long match, you must work hard, never let up, and keep the pressure on at all times. As you wear your opponent down his serve will begin to falter, he will become slower at getting into proper position, and he will begin to make more errors.

If a player is known to have a strong, consistent overhead smash it is only logical to attempt passing shots down the sidelines when that player is at the net. Lobs should be used occasionally to keep an opponent off balance and force him away from the net.

4. *What is the attitude and temperament of an opponent? How will my pattern of play affect him?* It is helpful to anticipate how an opponent will react to different patterns of play. For example, some players react to a net rusher by methodically taking all the time possible to hit down the line or lob. Others feel pressure from a net rusher and begin to hurry their shots, to glance at the opponent rather than concentrate on the ball, and eventually begin to make errors.

Players also react differently to lobs. Whereas one player may return one lob after another with precision, other players may return only a few lobs before gradually losing their timing and possibly their composure.

Some players react to the pressure of being behind by becoming more aggressive. Others "tighten up." The nervousness they feel is apparent as they become overly cautious with their hits and either err or repeatedly execute poorly placed returns or have such little pace they allow the opponent to hit the winning shots.

Pressure can sometimes be applied to an opponent simply by being in the best possible position for every hit. As a player realizes his opponent is in position for every return, he is under pressure to make his hits better—harder, closer to the lines, into the corners, etc.—and again the chance for error increases.

5. *How will my pattern of play affect my physical ability?* Attempting to put pressure on an opponent by rushing the net extensively requires excellent physical conditioning. It might be possible for a player to maintain the pace for one or two sets without adequate conditioning, but it is doubtful whether this pattern of play could be maintained throughout a match.

A player may realize that the speed of his serve is difficult for a particular opponent to handle and that he can win many points on the serve alone. He must consider, however, that the "big serve" requires a greater expenditure of energy than does a slower serve. He must decide whether he has sufficient stamina to force an opponent continually with hard serves or whether he must conserve his strength. At times it may be necessary to lessen the power of a serve and rely on getting the first serve into play. Having to serve the second ball necessitates nearly twice the expenditure of energy merely to put the ball in play.

AFTER READING THIS CHAPTER, YOU SHOULD NOW REALIZE:

The importance of the various advanced strokes and their effectiveness in a given situation.

That each player's position on the court, in both singles and doubles, depends on his ability and on whether or not he feels comfortable at the net.

That, for the novice at least, a basic rule of strategy is to keep the ball in play.

That percentage tennis is the ability to hit the shot or pattern of shots that provides the greatest chance of winning the point.

GLOSSARY OF TERMS

Ace: A legal serve so successful that the receiver is unable to touch it.

Advantage: The point following a score of deuce. Advantage or "ad" in means that the server has won the point; "ad" out means that the receiver has won the point.

All: Term used to indicate tie scores, for example, 15 *all* or 30 *all*.

Alley: Area between the singles and doubles side lines that forms part of the doubles court.

American twist: Variety of serve that puts forward and sideward spin on the ball causing a high bounce, usually to the receiver's backhand.

Approach shot: A ball returned deep into the opponent's court allowing the hitter to move forward from the baseline to a position at the net.

Backcourt: Area of the court between the base line and the service line.

Backcourt game: A style of play in which a player remains on or just behind the base line rather than at the net.

Backhand: Any ball a right handed player hits from his left side or a left handed player hits from his right side.

Backspin: Spin that causes the ball to rotate counter-clockwise to its line of movement.

Base line: The lines forming the back boundaries of a tennis court.

Center mark: The mark bisecting the mid-point of the base line separating the right and left sides of the court, indicating proper areas from which to serve.

Center service line: The line extending down the center of the court from the net to the service line, separating the right and left service courts.

Chip shot: Short shot angled toward the side lines; frequently used on the service return in doubles.

Chop: Stroke in which the racket is drawn downward as the ball is hit, imparting backspin.

Cross court: A ball hit from the corner or side of one court *diagonally* across the net to the opposite corner or side.

Davis Cup Matches: International competition among teams of men representing the competing countries.

Deep: Indicates a ball hit near the base line or, on a serve, near the service line.

Deuce: Term indicating an even score when each player has won three points, or an even number of points thereafter.

Double fault: Failure to legally serve the ball into the proper service court on either of two allotted tries; results in loss of point.

Doubles: Play in which two teams of two players each compete.

Drive: Ball hit with little arc from a point near the base line, landing deep in the opponent's backcourt.

Drop shot: Ball is hit with backspin, barely clears the net, and drops to the opponent's court near the net with little bounce.

Drop volley: A stroke similar to a drop shot but executed from a volley rather than a drive.

Error: A point lost because of a mistake rather than through an opponent's placement or good play.

Even court: The right service court. When service is directed to the receiver's right service court, an even number of points has been completed in the game. This court is also referred to as the forehand court.

Fault: Failure to legally serve the ball into the proper service court.

Federation Cup Matches: International competition among teams of women representing the competing countries.

Fifteen: First point won in a tennis game.

Flat: A ball hit with little or no spin.

Foot fault: Serve ruled illegal because server stepped on the base line or into the court before his racket contacted the ball; can also result from illegal motions with the feet prior to or during the serve.

Forecourt: Portion of the court between the service line and the net.

Forehand: Any ball a right handed player hits from his right side or a left handed player hits from his left side.

Forty: Score of a player who has won three points.

Game: Unit of scoring. Winning player must have at least four points and be at least two points ahead of his opponent.

Grand slam: Winning the United States, Australian, French, and English (Wimbledon) national championships in one season.

Half volley: A defensive stroke in which the ball is hit immediately after it bounces. It is usually because player has failed to achieve a volleying position.

ILTF: International Lawn Tennis Federation.

Let: A served ball that hits the net but falls into the proper service court; the ball must be served again. "Let" also refers to a point that must be re-played.

Lob: A ball hit in a high arc, landing near the opponent's base line. The basic purpose of a lob is to keep the ball out of reach of the net man.

Love: A score of zero in a game; also denotes a set score of zero.

Match: A unit of scoring. Winner has taken two of three sets or three of five sets.

Mixed doubles: A doubles game in which a man and woman are partners against another man and woman.

Net game: Play at or near the net consisting largely of volleys and overhead smashes.

Odd court: The left service court. When service is directed to the receiver's left service court, an uneven number of points has been completed. Also referred to as the backhand court.

Overhead smash: An offensive stroke similar to the serve. A high ball is hit in a hard downward path. Also referred to as a "smash."

Passing shot: Ball is hit past the reach of a net player, down either side or cross court.

Placement: Ball is directed to a specific area of the court where the opponent has difficulty returning it.

Racket face: Surface formed by the strings of a tennis racket; the hitting surface.

Rally: The act of hitting the ball back and forth over the net during the warm up or following the serve.

Rough or smooth: Refers to the small trimming strings at the top and bottom of the racket face that are used when spinning the racket to determine the choice of serving or receiving and the selection of each player's side of the court. The trim string is looped around a main string giving a rough surface to one side and a smooth surface to the opposite side.

Serve: The stroke used to put the ball in play at the beginning of each point.

Service break: Winning a game your opponent has served. Skilled players usually win their serves and attempt to "break" their opponent's serve.

Service line: Line parallel with the base line, separating the right and left service courts from the backcourt.

Set: A unit of scoring completed when one player has won at least six games and is two or more games ahead of his opponent.

Sidelines: Outer boundary lines perpendicular to the net and extending from base line to base line. The singles sidelines define the singles court; the doubles sidelines, the doubles court.

Singles: Play in which one player competes against a single opponent.

Slice: Stroke in which racket movement puts spin on the ball. The term usually refers to backspin or lateral spin on drives and to lateral spin on serves.

Spinning the racket: Method of determining (1) which player or team will begin serving, and (2) the side of the court on which each player or team will begin. The racket tip is placed on the ground, the racket is spun and allowed to fall, as in flipping a coin.

Thirty: A player's second point in a game.

Topspin: The racket brushes up and over the back of the ball, causing it to rotate forward or clockwise in relation to its line of movement.

USLTA: United States Lawn Tennis Association. The official tennis governing body in the United States.

Volley: Hitting a ball in mid air before it has bounced.

Wightman Cup Matches: Women's team competition between the United States and England.

Wimbledon: Home of the All England Tennis Championships; the world's largest open tournament.

BIBLIOGRAPHY

Bradfield, Robert B. 1968. The relative importance of physical activity for the overweight. *Nutrition News,* 31:13-14.

Buchanan, Lamont. 1951. *The story of tennis.* New York: The Vanguard Press.

Cooper, John M., and Glassow, Ruth B. 1968. *Kinesiology.* St. Louis: The C. V. Mosby Co.

Cooper, Kenneth H. 1968. *Aerobics.* New York: M. Evans and Co.

Cowell, Charles C. 1960. The contributions of physical activity to social development. *Research Quarterly,* 31:286-305.

Cratty, Bryant J. 1964. *Movement behavior and motor learning.* Philadelphia: Lea and Febiger.

Hein, Fred V., and Ryan, Allen J. 1960. The contributions of physical activity to physical health. *Research Quarterly,* 31:263-85.

Hilgard, E. R., and Atkinson, R. C. 1967. *Introduction to psychology.* New York: Harcourt, Brace and World, Inc.

Jones, C. M. 1969. The championships rebound from global war. *Tennis USA,* 32:28-30.

Kozar, J. J., and Hunsicker, Paul. 1963. A study of telemetered heart rate during sports participation of young adult men. *Journal of Sports Medicine and Physiological Fitness,* 3:1.

Mayer, Jean. 1967. *Weight control.* Freeport, New York: Educational Activities Inc.

McDonald, Frederick J. 1965. *Educational psychology.* Belmont, Calif.: Wadsworth Publishing Co., Inc.

Meninger, W. C. 1948. Recreation and mental health. *Recreation,* 42:340.

Nikolic, Sima. 1970. The history of intercollegiate tennis at Brigham Young University. Unpublished master's thesis, Brigham Young University, 1970.

Official USLTA yearbook and tennis guide, 1970. 475 Fifth Ave., New York: H. O. Zimman Co., Inc.

Oxendine, Joseph B. 1968. *Psychology of motor learning*. New York: Appleton-Century-Crofts.

Robb, Margaret. 1966. Feedback. *Quest*, 6:38-42.

Scott, M. Gladys. 1960. The contributions of physical activity to psychological development. *Research Quarterly*, 31:307-20.

Sharkey, Brian J., and Holleman, John P. 1967. Cardio-respiratory adaptations to training at specific intensities. *Research Quarterly,* 38:698-704.

Skubic, Vera, and Hodgkins, Jean. 1967. Relative strenuousness of selected sports as performed by women. *Research Quarterly*, 38:305-13.

Widule, Carol J. 1968. Physical laws and human structure, in *Introduction to human movement*. ed., Hope M. Smith. Reading, Mass.: Addison-Wesley Publishing Co.

INDEX